THE RESONANT MARKETS SERIES

Decoding the Human Nature of Market Moves

How Emotions Drive Financial Markets

Deepanshu Suman

2025 — First Edition

Master Market Psychology, Outsmart the Crowd, Trade with Confidence

Copyright

Title: Decoding the Human Nature of Market Moves
Author: Deepanshu Suman

First Edition
ISBN: 978-93-344-4649-4

Disclaimer: This book is intended for educational and informational purposes only. It explores market psychology, behavioral patterns, and human nature in financial decision-making. It is not professional financial, investment, legal, or personal advice. Readers should consult qualified professionals before acting on any information presented herein.

All brand names, trademarks, product names, and company names mentioned are the property of their respective owners. References are included solely for illustrative, educational, or informational purposes and do not imply any affiliation, endorsement, or sponsorship by those brands or entities. The author does not claim ownership of any referenced brand, trademark, or content.

Dedication

To all traders, investors, and curious minds who dare to look beyond charts and numbers, seeking to understand the human forces that drive markets. This book is for those who embrace uncertainty and strive to master themselves as much as the markets they navigate.

Acknowledgements

I am deeply grateful to the mentors, colleagues, and thought leaders who shaped my understanding of market psychology and human behavior. Special thanks to my family and friends for their unwavering support, patience, and encouragement throughout the journey of writing this book. I also extend my appreciation to the countless traders, both professional and retail, whose experiences, stories, and mistakes informed the insights shared here. Your courage to act, reflect, and learn continues to inspire this work.

Preface

Financial markets are far more than charts, numbers, and algorithms they are mirrors reflecting the collective behavior, emotions, and decisions of millions of participants. Every rally, crash, or unexpected swing in price is not merely a result of data or fundamentals, but the visible outcome of invisible human forces. This book is my attempt to decode those forces, to explore how human nature shapes market moves, and to provide a framework for understanding both the markets and your own responses within them.

Why This Book is Different

Most trading and investing books focus narrowly on technical indicators, strategies, or fundamental analysis, often ignoring the critical element that drives all market action: human behavior. This book takes a different approach. It blends insights from behavioral finance, psychology, and evolutionary biology with real-world trading examples to reveal why markets often behave irrationally, why trends can persist beyond logic, and why even experienced traders fall prey to emotional biases.

You will learn to identify patterns not just in prices but in behavior your own and that of the broader market. From understanding fear, greed, and overconfidence to recognizing the subtle signals of the crowd, this book provides both conceptual understanding and practical tools to navigate complex market dynamics. Unlike conventional guides, the goal here is not only to teach you what to trade, but to teach you how to think, decide, and act under uncertainty.

Who It's For: Traders, Investors, and Curious Minds

This book is designed for a wide audience: traders seeking a psychological edge, investors wanting to understand the forces behind market cycles, and curious minds fascinated by the intersection of human behavior and finance. Whether you are a beginner struggling with emotional decisions, an experienced trader aiming to refine your mindset, or a professional investor seeking deeper insight into market psychology, you will find value in these pages. The lessons here extend beyond finance they are relevant to decision-making, risk management, and understanding human behavior in complex systems.

How to Read This Book

This book is designed to be both a conceptual guide and a practical toolkit. To get the most value, it is important to understand how the content is structured and how to interpret the symbols, charts, and actionable tips included throughout.

Reading Approach

You can approach this book in multiple ways:

- **Sequential Reading:** Follow the chapters in order to build a step-by-step understanding of market psychology from foundational principles to strategic applications.
- **Targeted Reading:** Jump to sections that address your current challenges, questions, or areas of interest. Each part is designed to stand on its own, with clear context and explanations.
- **Practical Application:** Keep a trading or observation journal alongside your reading. Record your emotional reactions, decisions, and insights as you apply the concepts to real or simulated market scenarios.

Symbols and Notation

Throughout this book, certain symbols and formatting conventions are used to highlight key ideas:

- **Actionable Insight:** Highlights practical strategies or exercises you can implement immediately.
- **Charts and Visuals:** Illustrations of market patterns, cycles, emotional waves, and archetypes. These are tools to help you visualize concepts and connect theory to real-world behavior.

- **Reflection Prompt:** Questions designed to encourage self-awareness and introspection. These prompts help you recognize personal biases and emotional patterns in your own trading or investing.
- **Key Takeaway:** Summarizes the most important points of a section for quick reference and reinforcement.

Charts and Visual Aids

Charts, graphs, and diagrams are included to:

- Illustrate recurring emotional cycles and market phases.
- Demonstrate behavioral patterns of different market participants.
- Provide a visual framework for probabilistic thinking and decision-making.

These visuals are not just decorative they are intended to help you internalize concepts, anticipate market behavior, and recognize patterns as they unfold.

Actionable Tips

Each chapter contains actionable tips and exercises designed to bridge theory and practice. These include:

- Journaling exercises to track emotional reactions and biases.
- Observational tasks to identify crowd behavior and sentiment in real markets.
- Practical strategies for decision-making under uncertainty and risk.

By actively engaging with these tips, you will transform understanding into skill, building both psychological resilience and a practical edge in trading and investing.

Key Terms

Before diving into the core concepts, it's important to become familiar with the key terms, abbreviations, and concepts that appear throughout this book. Understanding these terms will help you navigate the material with ease, especially when dealing with market structure, psychology, and institutional trading language.

Core Market Terms

- **Liquidity:** The ease with which assets can be bought or sold without causing significant price movement. In smart money terms, liquidity often represents clusters of stop-loss orders or pending positions.
- **Market Structure:** The framework of price movement, including highs, lows, trends, and consolidations, that defines how the market transitions between accumulation, manipulation, and distribution phases.
- **Order Block (OB):** A zone where institutional orders have been placed usually before a major price move. Often serves as key support or resistance.
- **Fair Value Gap (FVG):** The imbalance between buyers and sellers left on a chart when price moves aggressively, often signaling potential retracement zones.
- **Stop Hunt:** A move designed to trigger stop-loss orders and capture liquidity before the market reverses direction.
- **Smart Money:** Refers to institutional traders banks, hedge funds, and market makers whose actions often lead market direction.
- **Retail Traders:** Individual or small-scale traders who typically react to price rather than anticipate it, often providing liquidity to institutional strategies.

Psychological and Behavioral Terms

- **Cognitive Bias:** Systematic errors in thinking that affect trading decisions such as overconfidence, loss aversion, and confirmation bias.
- **Emotional Cycle of Markets:** The recurring psychological stages optimism, euphoria, anxiety, denial, panic, and hope that drive crowd behavior.
- **Probabilistic Thinking:** The mindset of evaluating outcomes in terms of probabilities rather than certainties an essential skill for long-term trading success.
- **Recency Bias:** The tendency to give more weight to recent experiences or outcomes when making trading decisions.
- **FOMO (Fear of Missing Out):** The emotional urge to enter trades impulsively when price moves without participation, often leading to poor entries.
- **Discipline:** The ability to follow a defined plan or process despite emotional impulses or short-term market noise.

Common Abbreviations

- **SMC:** Smart Money Concepts a framework for analyzing market behavior through institutional perspectives.
- **ICT:** Inner Circle Trader a methodology and educational approach emphasizing institutional order flow and liquidity theory.
- **OB:** Order Block.
- **FVG:** Fair Value Gap.
- **PD Array:** Premium/Discount Array zones of value where institutions look for entries in alignment with market structure.
- **HTF / LTF:** Higher Time Frame / Lower Time Frame used to distinguish between macro and micro perspectives in analysis.
- **RR:** Risk-to-Reward Ratio the ratio of potential profit to potential loss in a trade setup.
- **SL / TP:** Stop Loss / Take Profit pre-defined levels to exit a trade automatically.
- **MM:** Market Maker institutional participant responsible for providing liquidity and maintaining orderly markets.
- **BB:** Breaker Block a failed order block that shifts market structure.

Key Conceptual Distinctions

- **Price vs. Value:** Price is what you pay; value is what institutions seek to exploit through inefficiencies.
- **Liquidity vs. Volatility:** Liquidity represents participation; volatility represents displacement. High volatility does not always mean high liquidity.
- **Emotion vs. Logic:** Emotional trades are reactive; logical trades are rule-based and probabilistic.
- **Information vs. Insight:** Information is abundant; insight comes from understanding human behavior behind the data.

Tip for Readers

If you're new to trading or market psychology, consider bookmarking this section. You'll find yourself returning here as you progress through the book and encounter new concepts. Each chapter builds on these foundational terms, deepening your understanding of how markets and traders truly operate.

Contents

Part I

Why Human Nature Rules the Market

Chapter 1

The Invisible Hand of Emotion

Before algorithms, before Bloomberg terminals, and long before technical indicators cluttered our charts, the market was moved by one thing emotion. Even today, behind every candle, every breakout, and every crash, there is a heartbeat. Markets may speak in numbers, but their language is written in human psychology.

Imagine a trader sitting at their desk late at night, staring at a position that's a few points away from stop loss. Logic says "hold your plan," but fear whispers, "get out before it's too late." Across the world, thousands of traders feel the same pulse of panic. Together, their collective decision to exit turns a small dip into a cascade. The chart moves not because of news, not because of data but because of emotion made visible.

The market is a mirror, and what it reflects most clearly is our collective state of mind. Greed stretches price beyond reason; fear drags it below value. Euphoria builds bubbles, despair creates bottoms. Fundamentals may define what something is worth, but emotion determines when that worth is recognized or ignored.

This chapter explores the hidden force shaping every price move: the psychology that drives buying and selling decisions. We'll see how crowd behavior often overwhelms rational analysis, why fundamentals alone can't predict timing, and how the paradox of "rational irrationality" defines every modern market. Once you understand that prices are emotions quantified, you'll begin to see what most traders never do the human fingerprint behind every tick.

1.1 How Psychology Shapes Price Action

If markets are reflections of collective human behavior, then price action is the visible pulse of that behavior. Every rise and fall, every candle and consolidation, represents countless individual emotions fear, greed, hope, denial aggregated into one moving number. Understanding how psychology shapes price is not philosophy; it's practicality. The market is not a mystery when seen as an emotional organism.

The Market as a Behavioral Machine

Price action is not random noise it is structured human emotion expressed through orders. When traders buy, they are expressing belief, confidence, or fear of missing out. When they sell, they are expressing doubt, anxiety, or fear of loss. The market, therefore, behaves like a behavioral machine that translates internal human states into external price movements.

Every tick is an outcome of millions of tiny emotional impulses. Prices rise not because of "facts" but because a majority feels optimistic enough to pay a higher price. Prices fall not because value disappears but because collective confidence does. Charts, in this sense, are emotional signatures plotted through time.

Belief, Expectation, and Perception

Markets do not move on reality they move on the perception of reality. Traders and investors act not on what *is*, but on what they *believe will be.* The disconnect between fact and expectation is where opportunity and chaos lives.

- **Belief:** Every trade reflects an underlying belief about value or probability. "This stock will rise," "the Fed will pause," "the AI boom will last."
- **Expectation:** Once a belief is shared widely, it becomes priced in. A positive earnings report can trigger a sell-off not because it's bad, but because it wasn't better than expected.
- **Perception:** Market prices are the weighted average of all perceptions rational and irrational alike. As perceptions shift, prices adjust instantly.

This dynamic means that markets are always discounting the future not as it will be, but as humans *expect* it to be. When collective expectation overshoots, bubbles form. When despair overshoots, bottoms emerge.

Emotion as Market Energy

Think of emotion as the energy that fuels price movement. When optimism dominates, demand for risk increases, liquidity expands, and prices trend upward. When fear dominates, liquidity evaporates, risk tolerance collapses, and prices fall sharply.

Greed and fear are not opposites they are phases of the same emotional spectrum. The same dopamine circuits that drive ambition in a bull market drive panic in a crash. Both stem from a single primitive mechanism: survival. Traders chase reward and flee pain just as our ancestors chased food and fled predators. The market merely translates these instincts into financial form.

Feedback Loops and Reflexivity

Price itself feeds back into psychology. Rising prices make people feel wealthier and more confident, prompting more buying reinforcing the trend. Falling prices trigger fear and regret, prompting more selling accelerating the decline. This reflexive feedback loop between price and emotion is what turns rational expectations into irrational extremes.

George Soros described this phenomenon as *reflexivity*: perceptions influence reality, which in turn alters perceptions. In markets, this means that emotion doesn't just respond to price it creates it. Bubbles inflate and burst because emotion amplifies its own signal until the system collapses under its weight.

Cognitive Biases That Distort Price

Even the most experienced traders are not immune to cognitive distortions mental shortcuts that evolved for survival, not speculation. These biases create predictable patterns in price action.

- **Loss Aversion:** People feel the pain of loss twice as strongly as the pleasure of gain. This leads to holding losers too long and cutting winners too early.
- **Confirmation Bias:** Traders seek information that validates their current belief and ignore evidence that contradicts it. This sustains trends longer than fundamentals justify.
- **Herding Effect:** Seeing others profit creates FOMO. People imitate what seems to work, amplifying moves into bubbles and crashes.
- **Recency Bias:** The most recent experience dominates memory. A few weeks of rally can erase memories of bear markets, leading to complacency.
- **Anchoring:** Traders fixate on arbitrary reference points like entry price or last high and make decisions around them, even when irrelevant.

Each bias contributes to price anomalies momentum runs, overreactions, false breakouts that form the rhythm of market behavior. Recognizing these biases doesn't eliminate them, but it helps you identify when the crowd is collectively falling into their trap.

The Crowd Mind and Emotional Contagion

Markets are not a collection of isolated individuals; they are social systems. Emotion spreads through them like a virus. One trader's fear, expressed through a stop-loss or market sell, triggers another's anxiety, and soon panic becomes contagious. Similarly, excitement spreads through bullish narratives, social media, and success stories creating collective euphoria.

This "crowd mind" explains why rational individuals can produce irrational markets. The emotional contagion creates synchronized behavior herding, panic selling, parabolic rallies that can only be understood through group psychology, not individual logic.

Price as a Storytelling Mechanism

Humans understand the world through stories, and markets are no exception. Every rally or crash has a narrative: "AI is the future," "inflation is dead," "this time is different." These stories give traders emotional permission to act. They simplify uncertainty into conviction.

But narratives are fragile. When the story breaks when new data contradicts belief the emotional unwinding can be violent. The stronger the narrative, the harder its collapse. Understanding which stories dominate the market is as critical as reading the chart itself.

The Neuroscience of Trading Behavior

From a neuroscientific view, trading behavior is driven by two competing systems: the *reward system* (dopamine) and the *threat system* (cortisol).

- When markets rise, dopamine creates excitement and risk-seeking. The brain associates anticipation with reward, often before the gain even happens.
- When markets fall, cortisol floods the body, shrinking time perception and pushing decision-making toward instinct fight, flight, or freeze.

This biological rhythm creates the alternating waves of greed and fear seen in every market cycle. Mastering markets, therefore, requires mastering your physiology not just your analysis.

Emotions Leave Footprints on Charts

The beauty of price action is that it records emotion objectively. Certain chart patterns are the visual fingerprints of collective feeling:

- **Panic Selling:** Sharp vertical drops with huge volume show mass capitulation.

- **Euphoric Tops:** Steep, unsustainable rallies with crowd exuberance mark greed at its peak.
- **False Breakouts:** Emotional overreactions trigger stop hunts before price snaps back to equilibrium.
- **Sideways Ranges:** Periods of confusion, indecision, and psychological balance between opposing forces.

Reading charts through this emotional lens transforms them from static lines into dynamic human stories.

Turning Awareness into Edge

Recognizing the psychological nature of markets isn't just philosophy it's a trading advantage. When you learn to see how emotion drives order flow, you stop fighting randomness and start interpreting rhythm. You understand that volatility is not chaos, but the natural language of sentiment shifts.

A practical approach is to:

- Journal your emotional state before and after trades.
- Track sentiment indicators like put-call ratios, VIX, or retail positioning.
- Observe when news triggers exaggerated price moves they often signal emotional excess.
- Identify when the crowd is leaning too heavily in one direction; the reversal often begins not with logic, but with exhaustion.

Actionable Insight: The next time you analyze a chart, ask yourself "What emotion is this price expressing right now?" Fear, greed, hope, regret? Once you can read that, you're no longer trading charts; you're trading human nature.

Conclusion: The Mind Behind Every Move

Psychology doesn't just influence price it is price. What moves markets is not information, but interpretation; not data, but emotion. The laws of supply and demand are real, but they are filtered through human perception, and perception is never neutral.

To master markets, therefore, is to master the emotional code beneath them. When you begin to see charts as living records of collective behavior, you stop asking "What will happen?" and start asking "What are people feeling?" That's where real market understanding begins.

1.2 Why Fundamentals Often Lose to Feelings

While academic models rely on fundamentals, markets are supposed to be efficient machines constantly processing new information and reflecting it perfectly in price. In the real world, markets are more like emotional organisms. They breathe, they panic, they celebrate. Prices swing not only because of balance sheets or interest rates, but because millions of human minds are trying to make sense of uncertainty, together, in real time.

The truth is uncomfortable but undeniable: in the short to medium term, fundamentals often lose to feelings. The market, being a collective expression of human psychology, reacts far more to perception, emotion, and narrative than to raw data. It is not the facts that move prices it is how those facts are felt.

The Emotional Operating System of Markets

Every trader, investor, and algorithm operates on inputs. For humans, those inputs are filtered through an emotional lens shaped by fear, greed, and cognitive bias. Behavioral economists like Daniel Kahneman and Richard Thaler have shown that even the most "rational" decision-makers are influenced by subconscious emotions. In markets, those tiny emotional deviations when multiplied across millions of participants create huge deviations in price.

Fear of missing out (FOMO) makes investors chase momentum; loss aversion makes them sell too soon or hold too long; confirmation bias makes them seek evidence that supports their existing beliefs. The market is not moved by spreadsheets, but by stories and every story that catches fire triggers a self-reinforcing feedback loop between price and emotion.

When prices rise, confidence grows. When confidence grows, more people buy. That buying pushes prices even higher, reinforcing the belief that the move was justified. The same logic works in reverse during crashes: falling prices breed panic, panic leads to selling, and the selling accelerates the fall. In both cases, feelings overwhelm fundamentals.

Why Fundamentals Struggle in the Short Term

Fundamentals describe reality; psychology describes perception. The gap between the two is where opportunity and chaos coexist. A company's intrinsic value might change slowly over quarters or years, but investor sentiment can shift in seconds. That's why you can have a profitable company whose stock plunges 30% overnight or a loss-making startup whose valuation multiplies tenfold in a year.

Markets do not price what *is*, but what people *believe will be*. And belief, unlike profit margins, is volatile.

Take Tesla, for example. For years, analysts debated its "true value." Traditional valuation metrics price-to-earnings, cash flow, debt ratios suggested overvaluation. Yet the stock soared as investors priced in Elon Musk's narrative of a clean-energy future and technological dominance. Belief, not balance sheets, drove that exponential growth. Similarly, during the crypto boom of 2020–2021, coins with no utility or cash flow reached billion-dollar valuations simply because collective enthusiasm overwhelmed skepticism. The story was stronger than the spreadsheet.

On the flip side, during crises like 2008 or March 2020 fundamentally strong companies saw their stock prices collapse, not because their value disappeared overnight, but because fear erased confidence. Investors sold anything that could be sold. Liquidity mattered more than logic. In those moments, emotion doesn't just distort price it defines it.

The Anatomy of Sentiment Waves

Market sentiment operates in cycles that are as psychological as they are financial:

1. **Disbelief:** A new trend begins, but few trust it. 2. **Hope:** Early believers enter, thinking "maybe this time is different." 3. **Euphoria:** Everyone wants in valuations detach from reality. 4. **Complacency:** Fundamentals are ignored; narratives dominate. 5. **Anxiety:** Prices stall; doubt creeps in. 6. **Denial:** Investors rationalize losses. 7. **Panic:** Fear explodes; selling becomes contagious. 8. **Capitulation:** Confidence collapses; assets are dumped indiscriminately. 9. **Depression:** Prices undershoot value; the crowd retreats. 10. **Hope (again):** The cycle restarts with new narratives and faces.

At every stage, fundamentals act like an anchor but the emotional tide pushes prices far above and below that anchor point.

The Neuroscience Behind Irrational Markets

To understand why feelings overpower logic, we must look at the human brain itself. Decision-making under uncertainty activates the limbic system the emotional brain more than the prefrontal cortex, which handles reasoning. When traders see green candles and rapid gains, dopamine floods the brain, producing a euphoric high similar to gambling wins. Conversely, when losses occur, the amygdala triggers stress hormones like cortisol, prompting fight-or-flight responses.

This neurochemical dance explains why traders often do the exact opposite of what logic dictates: buying at tops (chasing pleasure) and selling at bottoms (escaping pain). The brain was never designed for probabilistic decision-making it evolved to survive, not to compound wealth.

The Long-Term Redemption of Fundamentals

Over long horizons, fundamentals do eventually matter. Companies with real cash flows, durable moats, and prudent management tend to outperform narratives built on hype. Markets, though irrational in the short term, have a way of self-correcting over time as emotion cycles fade and capital redistributes toward efficiency.

But "eventually" can take years. As John Maynard Keynes famously said, *"The market can remain irrational longer than you can remain solvent."* Traders and investors who ignore sentiment in favor of pure logic risk being crushed by waves of emotion before the tide of fundamentals returns.

The Takeaway: Emotion Is the First Mover

Price does not wait for earnings reports or annual statements it reacts to emotion first, logic later. Fundamentals set the destination; psychology determines the journey. Understanding this hierarchy is vital. The best traders do not fight the crowd's feelings; they read them, ride them, and exit before the mood changes.

In the marketplace of human emotion, fundamentals provide the compass, but feelings steer the ship.

1.3 The Paradox: Markets Are Rationally Irrational

At first glance, the phrase "rationally irrational" sounds like a contradiction. How can markets that depend on human emotion and bias often bordering on chaos still produce long-term order and growth? Yet this paradox is the essence of market behavior. It is precisely because humans are predictably emotional that markets, as collective systems, function in a strangely rational way over time.

The Myth of the Rational Market

Traditional economics paints markets as efficient, rational systems that instantaneously reflect all available information. This is the core of the Efficient Market Hypothesis (EMH), a theory comforting in its simplicity and elegance. But step into any trading floor, online forum, or retail chat group during a bull run, and the illusion shatters.

People are not rational calculators they are storytellers, gamblers, and emotional herd animals. Prices overshoot, narratives dominate, and bubbles form not because of hidden information, but because of shared emotion.

Yet, here's the twist: despite all this apparent madness, the market as a whole still trends upward across centuries. Amidst countless manias and crashes, progress persists. Irrationality, when aggregated and recycled through competition, somehow produces rational long-term outcomes.

Rationality at the Macro, Irrationality at the Micro

Markets are composed of individuals each driven by bias, fear, greed, and self-interest. Individually, traders are irrational. Collectively, they are self-correcting.

When one group overreacts, another sees opportunity. When euphoria drives prices too high, rational arbitrageurs or cautious investors step in to short or sell. When panic drives prices too low, value seekers accumulate. These opposing forces, though slow and uneven, form the market's stabilizing feedback loop.

The market's "invisible hand," as Adam Smith described, is not cold logic it is the sum of countless emotional impulses that, when averaged, create balance. This is the genius of collective irrationality: it is chaotic at the micro level but structured at the macro level.

Think of it like a swarm of birds. Each bird moves unpredictably, but the flock, as a whole, forms a coherent pattern.

Emotions as a Feature, Not a Flaw

Human emotion is not a market defect it is the market's engine. Without fear, there would be no risk management; without greed, no innovation or speculation; without hope, no capital formation.

Every major bull market begins with optimism an emotional state, not a spreadsheet metric. Every crash begins with fear, the primal instinct of survival. Both are necessary for the cyclical renewal of markets.

When investors overvalue optimism, markets expand and innovate. When fear takes over, excesses are cleared, and the system resets. These alternating emotional tides create the market's rhythm expansion, contraction, and recovery. The market, in this sense, is rational not because its participants are logical, but because its cycles driven by emotion serve an evolutionary function. They purge inefficiency, reward adaptability, and restore equilibrium.

The Predictability of Irrationality

Paradoxically, because human irrationality is consistent, it becomes predictable. Greed always looks the same: overconfidence, leverage, "this time is different." Fear always follows: denial, panic, liquidation.

This predictability allows skilled traders and investors to anticipate turning points not by analyzing balance sheets, but by studying sentiment and behavior. The contrarian who buys when fear peaks, or sells when euphoria dominates, is not defying the market's logic but understanding it at a deeper, psychological level.

Behavioral patterns anchoring, loss aversion, overconfidence, herd mentality repeat endlessly, across centuries and asset classes. The same mental scripts that fueled the South Sea Bubble in the 1700s also drove the dot-com mania, the crypto frenzy, and the AI stock surge. The cast changes, but the psychology does not.

The Market as a Self-Learning Organism

Markets evolve not because participants become rational, but because systems adapt around their irrationality. Regulations tighten after crises, risk models improve, technology accelerates information flow, and capital moves faster. Yet, no matter how advanced the algorithms or AI trading systems become, they are still designed, calibrated, and trained on data created by humans data that reflects emotion.

Even machines inherit our irrational fingerprints. Algorithms may dampen noise, but they cannot erase fear and greed; they simply translate it into faster feedback loops. Flash crashes, meme stock rallies, and crypto manias are not signs of machine rationality they are proof that even automation amplifies human psychology.

The Beauty of the Paradox

The paradox of the market is this: it is an emotional battlefield that, over time, behaves like a rational ecosystem. It crashes, burns, rebuilds, and grows stronger. Every cycle of irrational exuberance and despair refines capital allocation, improves resilience, and rewards adaptability. The market is irrational in the moment but rational in the long arc of time.

This is why traders who focus solely on logic often fail, while those who understand emotion thrive. The market is not a machine to be solved it is a living mirror to be read.

Actionable Insight

Study the crowd, not just the company. Understand that emotion, not information, moves price in the short term. Learn to see panic and euphoria as signals, not noise. Mastering markets begins not with eliminating emotion, but with decoding it.

Chapter 2

Human Nature Human Behavior

Markets are shaped not just by what people do, but by why they do it. To navigate them effectively, we must distinguish between two closely related but fundamentally different concepts: human nature and human behavior. While the terms are often used interchangeably, confusing them can lead to costly mistakes in trading and investing.

Human nature refers to the fixed, hardwired tendencies that all humans share instincts and emotional patterns that have been honed by evolution over millennia. Fear of loss, desire for reward, and herd instinct are examples of traits embedded in our neural circuitry. These traits are predictable, universal, and remarkably consistent across cultures and centuries.

Human behavior, on the other hand, is the adaptive expression of these underlying tendencies in response to circumstances, environment, and learning. While nature sets the stage, behavior is the performance. It is flexible, context-dependent, and influenced by education, experience, social norms, and personal psychology. In markets, behavior manifests as buying, selling, holding, or panicking and it can vary widely even among people with identical instincts.

Understanding the distinction between nature and behavior is crucial for interpreting market dynamics. Crowds act collectively, and patterns emerge not from randomness but from predictable emotional wiring interacting with adaptive responses to price, news, and sentiment. By observing behavior while keeping human nature in mind, traders gain the ability to anticipate crowd reactions, identify turning points, and spot opportunities that others miss.

2.1 Nature: Fixed Tendencies

Human nature is the invisible architecture underlying every decision, trade, and market reaction. Unlike behavior, which can adapt based on experience, culture, or circumstance, nature represents the hardwired psychological and emotional tendencies embedded in our brains over millennia of evolution. In financial markets, these tendencies are the silent forces that shape price action long before logic or fundamentals intervene.

The Core Instincts Driving Markets

Several core tendencies are particularly relevant for understanding market dynamics:

- **Loss Aversion:** Humans instinctively fear losses more than they value equivalent gains. This survival mechanism ensures caution in life-threatening situations, but in markets, it leads to panic selling, reluctance to realize losses, and the amplification of crashes.
- **Greed and Reward Seeking:** The pursuit of reward is equally powerful. Dopamine-driven anticipation of gains motivates risk-taking, speculation, and momentum chasing. Markets exploit this by offering intermittent reinforcement through volatility, news, and trends.
- **Herd Behavior:** As social animals, humans rely on group cues for survival. In trading, this manifests as imitation, momentum following, and fear-of-missing-out (FOMO) behaviors. Crowds amplify both upward and downward movements.
- **Overconfidence:** Evolution favors decisive action. Humans often overestimate their knowledge and control, believing they can predict outcomes. In markets, overconfidence drives leverage, aggressive positions, and repeated risk-taking even in the face of losses.
- **Short-Term Bias:** Our brains are wired to prioritize immediate rewards. In investing, this leads to overemphasis on short-term price moves, reaction to news cycles, and impatience with long-term strategies.

These instincts operate beneath conscious awareness and are remarkably consistent across individuals, cultures, and generations. They are the reason why patterns of fear and greed repeat from Tulip Mania to the dot-com bubble, from the 2008 financial crisis to crypto frenzies.

The Neuroscience of Fixed Tendencies

Market psychology is rooted in neurobiology. Emotional and instinctive responses occur in the limbic system, often before the rational prefrontal cortex has time to process information:

- **Fear responses:** Triggered by potential losses, activating cortisol and stress pathways, leading to rapid withdrawal or panic behavior.
- **Reward anticipation:** Dopamine surges during upward price moves, encouraging continued risk-taking and reinforcing buying behavior.
- **Social reinforcement:** Observing peers profit activates mirror neurons, amplifying herd behavior and emotional contagion.

These neural responses are universal, making market patterns predictable at the collective level even if individual decisions appear erratic.

Fixed Tendencies in Market Context

Fixed tendencies explain the repetitive nature of market cycles:

- During euphoric rallies, greed and overconfidence dominate. Investors pile into assets, often ignoring fundamentals.
- During downturns, fear and loss aversion take control. Selling becomes contagious, amplifying declines.
- Herd behavior ensures that individual instincts scale into collective market phenomena trends, bubbles, and crashes.

By recognizing these tendencies, traders and investors can anticipate crowd reactions. Prices are not random; they are emotional expressions of human nature. Understanding these instincts is the first step in decoding market psychology.

Why Nature Matters for Traders

Nature sets the baseline. No amount of technical skill, fundamental analysis, or algorithmic sophistication can override these hardwired tendencies in the short term. Success in markets comes not from eliminating emotion, but from observing it, respecting it, and learning to act in harmony with it.

In the next section, we will explore how these fixed tendencies are expressed through *behavior* the adaptive responses that translate instinct into action within real-world markets.

2.2 Behavior: Adaptive Responses

While human nature provides the underlying blueprint, behavior is the dynamic expression of that blueprint in response to circumstance, learning, and environment. Behavior is where the fixed instincts of human nature meet the unpredictable reality of markets. It is adaptive, context-sensitive, and shaped by both individual psychology and collective dynamics.

From Instinct to Action

Nature dictates what we feel; behavior dictates what we do with those feelings. For example:

- Fear of loss (nature) may manifest as panic selling during a market crash, or as cautious hedging in a well-prepared trader (behavior).
- Desire for reward (nature) may drive reckless speculation for some, while inspiring disciplined accumulation for others.
- Herd instinct (nature) may lead one investor to blindly follow the crowd, while another may exploit it by taking a contrarian position.

Behavior is the bridge between instinct and observable market activity. By studying patterns of behavior, traders gain insight into how collective emotions translate into price movements.

Adaptive Responses in Market Cycles

Behavior varies depending on context, market phase, and environmental cues:

- **Bull Markets:** Optimism amplifies buying behavior. Even rational investors may increase leverage or chase performance to avoid missing out.
- **Bear Markets:** Fear dominates. Even fundamentally strong assets may be sold indiscriminately as liquidity and emotion take precedence.
- **Sideways Markets:** Uncertainty triggers analysis paralysis. Traders may hesitate, miss opportunities, or rely on heuristics rather than deep analysis.

Recognizing these adaptive responses allows a trader to anticipate shifts in supply and demand, spot extremes, and position ahead of the crowd.

Behavior is Predictable But Context Matters

Although behavior is more flexible than nature, it is not random. Patterns of adaptive behavior repeat across cycles because they are rooted in the same fundamental instincts. Traders often exhibit predictable sequences: hesitation, confirmation-seeking, overreaction, and retracement. By observing these sequences, it is possible to anticipate short-term market swings and crowd reactions.

However, context shapes how these behaviors are expressed. Cultural norms, education, market structure, news, and technology all modulate behavior. For instance, retail traders in the crypto market react differently to volatility than institutional traders in equities. Understanding both instinct and context is essential for decoding market psychology.

Behavioral Archetypes in Trading

Human behavior in markets often manifests in recognizable archetypes:

- **The Chaser:** Reacts impulsively to momentum, often buying high and selling low.
- **The Analyzer:** Deliberates extensively, avoiding impulsive decisions but sometimes missing opportunities.
- **The Contrarian:** Uses crowd behavior as a signal to act opposite the prevailing sentiment.
- **The Adaptive Trader:** Balances instinct and analysis, responding fluidly to market context while managing emotion.

These archetypes are not fixed; a single trader may exhibit different behaviors depending on market conditions, time horizon, or emotional state. Recognizing both your own behavioral patterns and those of the crowd is a key component of strategic market engagement.

The Practical Edge of Understanding Behavior

Nature tells you why markets react; behavior tells you how they react. By observing adaptive behavior, traders can:

- Anticipate crowd reactions to news or trends.
- Identify overreactions and underreactions in price.
- Adjust position sizing and timing based on likely behavioral responses.
- Exploit predictable patterns of human psychology without assuming markets are rational.

In the next section, we will explore **why knowing the difference between human nature and behavior allows traders to predict crowd reactions**, providing a framework for interpreting market psychology at both micro and macro levels.

2.3 Why Knowing the Difference Predicts Crowd Reactions

Understanding the distinction between human nature and human behavior is not an abstract exercise it is one of the most powerful tools a trader or investor can have. Nature provides the predictable instincts; behavior provides the observable actions. By linking the two, we gain the ability to anticipate crowd psychology, market extremes, and potential reversals.

The Predictable Engine Behind Markets

Markets are, at their core, the aggregated outcome of millions of human decisions. Each decision is informed by nature (instinct) but expressed through behavior (adaptive response). When enough participants act in similar ways, patterns emerge trends, rallies, panics, and recoveries.

For example:

- A sudden drop in price may trigger fear (nature), leading to selling (behavior). Observing the acceleration of this behavior across participants signals the onset of panic, and potentially a market bottom.
- Rapid gains may trigger greed and overconfidence (nature), leading to momentum chasing (behavior). Watching the escalation of this behavior can indicate the peak of euphoria and the risk of a reversal.

The key insight is that behavior is the observable manifestation of underlying instincts. By studying behavior, we are essentially reading the emotional state of the market in real time.

Crowd Reactions as Behavioral Waves

Markets often move in predictable emotional waves because human nature is universal. Traders repeat the same biases, impulses, and mistakes across time and asset classes. The distinction between nature and behavior allows us to interpret these waves more accurately:

- **Fear-driven behavior:** Selling too early, panic liquidations, flight to safe assets.
- **Greed-driven behavior:** Speculative buying, over-leverage, ignoring fundamentals.
- **Herd behavior:** Following the majority, FOMO-driven entries, trend amplification.

Recognizing the difference between instinct and action lets traders identify which stage of the cycle the crowd is in, enabling better timing for entries and exits.

Practical Applications for Traders

1. **Sentiment Analysis:** Track behavior across markets, news, and social media to infer collective emotion. Understand that these behaviors stem from predictable instincts. 2. **Contrarian Opportunities:** When crowd behavior reflects extreme instincts panic, greed, or herd-driven mania look for asymmetric setups. 3. **Self-Awareness:** Compare your own behavior to your instincts. Are you acting out of fear or greed? Awareness of your own nature-behavior interplay helps you avoid common traps. 4. **Pattern**

Recognition: Repeated behavioral cycles manias, crashes, recoveries occur because human nature doesn't change. Identifying these cycles is more reliable than relying solely on fundamentals.

Historical Perspective

Consider the Dot-com bubble of 2000: nature's greed and herd instinct drove investors to chase every tech stock, behaviorally manifesting as speculative buying without regard for earnings. Similarly, during the 2008 crisis, fear and loss aversion led to widespread panic selling, behaviorally expressed as liquidity withdrawal and margin calls. Understanding that these behaviors stemmed from fixed human instincts would have allowed observers to anticipate extremes and position accordingly.

The Takeaway: Decode, Don't Fight

Markets are reflections of human emotion. Nature sets the stage; behavior enacts the drama. By separating the underlying instincts from their adaptive expressions, traders gain clarity. You do not need to predict every price move or control every variable. You only need to understand how the crowd's nature translates into behavior and when these behaviors are likely to reach their extremes.

In essence, knowing the difference between human nature and human behavior equips you with a predictive lens:

> *Observe behavior to read emotion; understand nature to anticipate it. Together, they reveal the crowd's likely next move.*

This framework is the foundation for all subsequent chapters, from crowd psychology and market cycles to trader mindset and strategic application. Mastery begins with understanding the difference between what humans feel and what humans do and the patterns that emerge when millions act together.

Chapter 3

The Market as a Mirror of the Mind

Markets are more than mechanisms for price discovery they are living, breathing reflections of human thought and emotion. Every candle, bar, and volume spike is a snapshot of collective psychology in action. When we study charts carefully, we are not just analyzing numbers; we are observing millions of individual decisions shaped by fear, hope, greed, and regret.

This chapter explores the idea that the market itself functions as a mirror, revealing the emotional states of the participants behind every trade. By understanding this concept, traders can move beyond mechanical analysis and start interpreting the underlying psychology driving price movements.

Patterns in the market are not random they are repeated emotional cycles. Just as human nature remains constant across generations, so too do the ways that emotions manifest in trading behavior. By recognizing these recurring cycles, we gain insight into potential market extremes, turning points, and periods of irrational exuberance or despair.

Sentiment waves movements of collective emotion play a crucial role in shaping price action. Fear can trigger panics, hope can inspire cautious accumulation, greed can drive unsustainable rallies, and regret can perpetuate hesitation or revenge trading. Understanding these waves, their triggers, and their behavioral signatures provides a framework for reading the market like a psychologist reads a human mind.

3.1 Every Chart is Collective Psychology Visualized

At first glance, a price chart may seem like nothing more than a sequence of numbers, candlesticks, or lines. Yet beneath these geometric shapes lies a far richer story: the emotions, decisions, and instincts of millions of market participants captured in real time. Every chart is, in essence, a mirror reflecting collective human psychology.

The Market as a Behavioral Canvas

Think of a chart as a canvas and traders as the artists. Each trade buy or sell is a brushstroke influenced by fear, greed, hope, or regret. When aggregated, these strokes form patterns, trends, and cycles that are visually recognizable. A sharp sell-off is not just a price drop; it is a wave of fear cascading through the market. A sustained rally is more than upward momentum; it is collective optimism and confidence crystallized in real time.

Volume, volatility, and price action are all psychological indicators disguised as technical data. Sudden spikes in volume reveal moments of mass decision-making; long wicks and tails in candlesticks hint at indecision or panic; consolidation periods reflect uncertainty or hesitation. By learning to interpret these signals, traders can read emotion directly from the market's visual language.

Why Charts Reflect Psychology, Not Just Fundamentals

Fundamental analysis explains why an asset might be valuable over the long term, but it rarely predicts the short-term path of price. That path is driven by human emotion: the crowd's reaction to news, rumors, earnings, or broader market sentiment. A strong earnings report may be ignored if fear dominates, while an insignificant rumor may trigger euphoria-fueled buying.

Charts capture these reactions with remarkable precision. Each candle represents a collective decision: who is confident, who is fearful, who is capitulating, who is accumulating. By studying charts through a psychological lens, traders gain insight into the underlying forces that move prices.

Recognizing Emotional Signatures in Charts

Certain recurring formations and movements can be directly linked to human psychology:

- **Sharp spikes and long tails:** Moments of panic or exuberance where emotions overwhelm rationality.
- **Consolidation and sideways movement:** Uncertainty, hesitation, or equilibrium between opposing emotional forces.
- **Breakouts and breakdowns:** Emotional tipping points where fear or greed becomes dominant.
- **Trend exhaustion and reversal patterns:** Collective regret or overconfidence reaching a limit, prompting a shift in behavior.

These signatures are universal they appear across asset classes, markets, and decades because human nature remains constant. What changes is context; what remains is predictable emotional behavior.

The Practical Edge

By viewing charts as mirrors of collective psychology rather than just price history:

- Traders can anticipate turning points before traditional indicators confirm them.
- They can separate noise from meaningful emotional signals.
- They can identify periods when crowd behavior is likely to exaggerate price moves, offering asymmetric opportunities.

In essence, every chart is a live map of human emotion in action. Understanding this transforms technical analysis from mere pattern recognition into a tool for reading the psychology of the market itself.

Key Insight

> *Charts do not lie they only reveal what humans collectively feel. To master markets, learn to see emotion in every line, every candle, and every spike.*

3.2 Patterns = Repeated Emotional Cycles

Markets are not random; they are rhythmic reflections of human emotion in motion. Just as individual behavior is shaped by instincts and adaptive responses, collective behavior creates recurring patterns cycles that repeat across time, assets, and geographies. Recognizing these cycles is a cornerstone of understanding market psychology.

The Emotional DNA of Market Patterns

Every market movement is rooted in fundamental human emotions: fear, hope, greed, and regret. These emotions do not manifest haphazardly they follow predictable sequences that repeat across time:

- **Hope:** Initial optimism or cautious accumulation sets the stage for a trend. Traders and investors begin to see potential gains and tentatively enter positions.
- **Greed:** As prices rise, confidence grows, and fear of missing out drives momentum buying. This is the phase where euphoria starts to dominate rational judgment.

- **Fear:** Eventually, reality or overextension triggers fear. Selling accelerates, profits are realized, and liquidity may dry up. Panic selling often follows as emotional contagion spreads.
- **Regret:** After a reversal, many feel regret for missed opportunities or for holding positions too long. This emotion influences subsequent behavior, shaping the next cycle.

These phases are universal, creating the cyclical patterns observed in charts, from rallies and corrections to bubbles and crashes.

Historical Evidence of Emotional Cycles

Consider several historical examples:

- **Tulip Mania (1630s):** Hope and greed drove unprecedented speculation in tulip bulbs, followed by fear and regret when prices collapsed.
- **Dot-com Bubble (late 1990s–2000):** Optimism in internet technology fueled greed-driven buying. Fear and regret dominated as valuations proved unsustainable, leading to dramatic reversals.
- **Cryptocurrency Rallies (2017, 2021):** Rapid accumulation, FOMO, and euphoria illustrate repeated emotional cycles across modern digital markets.

These examples highlight the timeless nature of emotional cycles they are not bound to a particular asset, era, or geography. Human nature ensures these patterns will continue to repeat.

Recognizing Cycles in Real Time

Traders can identify emotional cycles by observing:

- **Price acceleration:** Rapid moves often signal the greed phase.
- **Volatility spikes:** Sharp swings indicate fear or panic.
- **Volume surges:** High participation shows collective emotion reaching an extreme.
- **Behavioral indicators:** Sentiment surveys, social media trends, and positioning data reveal crowd psychology.

By mapping these signals, traders can anticipate turning points, avoid emotional traps, and exploit asymmetries created by overreactions.

Patterns as Predictive Tools

Understanding that patterns are emotional cycles transforms how traders approach markets:

- **Trend identification:** Recognize early-stage hope to enter positions with asymmetric upside.
- **Risk management:** Anticipate greed-driven euphoria to avoid over-exposure.
- **Contrarian opportunities:** Spot fear-induced sell-offs to identify potential market bottoms.

Rather than seeing charts as abstract figures, traders who understand patterns as emotional cycles read the story of collective psychology, allowing them to act proactively rather than reactively.

Key Insight

Market patterns are the footprints of human emotion. By learning to recognize these emotional cycles, traders can anticipate the crowd's next move before it becomes obvious in price.

3.3 Understanding Sentiment Waves: Fear, Hope, Greed, Regret

Markets move in waves of collective emotion. Just as the ocean has tides, markets have sentiment waves periods dominated by fear, hope, greed, and regret. These waves are the direct expression of human psychology on a massive scale, influencing every price movement, trend, and reversal. Understanding these waves is essential for interpreting market behavior and identifying trading opportunities.

Fear: The Market's Most Powerful Force

Fear is the emotion that drives sudden, extreme reactions. It can appear as panic selling, flight to safety, or liquidity withdrawal. Fear spreads quickly, often faster than rational analysis, because humans are wired to prioritize survival over opportunity.

- **Signs in the market:** Sharp declines, high volume on down days, widening bid-ask spreads, and heightened volatility indices (e.g., VIX).
- **Behavioral patterns:** Capitulation, herd selling, and risk aversion.
- **Trading implication:** Extreme fear often signals potential market bottoms or short-term oversold conditions. Traders who can recognize and act against panic can capitalize on opportunities while others flee.

Hope: The Seed of Recovery

Hope is subtler than fear but equally influential. It motivates accumulation and cautious optimism. Traders begin to re-enter positions, markets show early signs of stabilization, and sentiment shifts from pessimism toward belief in recovery.

- **Signs in the market:** Gradual upticks in price, stabilizing volume, and improved news sentiment.
- **Behavioral patterns:** Selective buying, accumulation by patient traders, and cautious optimism.
- **Trading implication:** Recognizing hope allows traders to position early in the initial stages of a recovery, capturing asymmetric upside before greed-driven momentum begins.

Greed: The Driver of Euphoria

Greed amplifies price moves and can create speculative bubbles. It emerges when gains reinforce confidence, and the fear of missing out (FOMO) dominates rational decision-making. Greed often peaks after a prolonged trend or rally.

- **Signs in the market:** Accelerated upward price movement, extreme valuations, high leverage, and euphoric media coverage.
- **Behavioral patterns:** Momentum buying, chasing returns, ignoring fundamentals, and overexposure to risk.
- **Trading implication:** Recognizing greed allows traders to protect profits, reduce exposure, and prepare for potential reversals driven by fear or regret.

Regret: The Lingering Emotional Aftermath

Regret follows losses, missed opportunities, or misjudgments. It can influence the next cycle by causing hesitation, revenge trading, or overcompensation.

- **Signs in the market:** Consolidation, sideways trading, or sudden counter-moves as participants react emotionally to past mistakes.
- **Behavioral patterns:** Hesitation, delayed participation, and attempts to "make up" for prior errors.
- **Trading implication:** Recognizing regret helps traders avoid emotionally driven decisions, stay disciplined, and act strategically rather than impulsively.

Reading and Using Sentiment Waves

To leverage sentiment waves effectively:

- Observe price action alongside volume and volatility to detect emotional extremes.
- Monitor news, social sentiment, and positioning data to gauge crowd psychology.
- Map the wave sequence fear, hope, greed, regret to anticipate potential turning points.
- Maintain self-awareness to distinguish your emotions from those of the crowd.

Key Insight

Sentiment waves are the heartbeat of the market. By learning to identify and interpret fear, hope, greed, and regret, traders gain a predictive edge seeing not just where the market has been, but where the crowd is likely to go next.

Chapter 4

Evolutionary Finance

Financial markets may seem like modern constructs of spreadsheets, algorithms, and electronic exchanges, but the forces that drive them are as old as humanity itself. Every decision to buy, sell, or hold is influenced by instincts shaped over hundreds of thousands of years responses that evolved to help our ancestors survive and thrive in uncertain environments. Evolutionary finance examines how these deep-rooted instincts manifest as biases in trading behavior, often leading to predictable patterns of error, overreaction, and opportunity.

This chapter explores the intersection of human evolution and market behavior. By understanding how survival wiring, reward anticipation, and social instincts influence decision-making, traders can recognize their own vulnerabilities and gain a strategic edge. We will examine why loss aversion dominates risk assessment, how dopamine and anticipation drive impulsive actions, and how recurring emotional loops can create both traps and opportunities in financial markets.

Through this lens, markets are not just arenas of rational calculation they are living laboratories where evolutionary instincts are expressed collectively, creating patterns that repeat across time and assets. By observing these instincts in action, you can learn to anticipate crowd behavior, manage your own impulses, and develop trading strategies that align with the underlying psychology of human nature.

4.1 How Hunter-Gatherer Instincts Became Trading Biases

To truly understand why traders behave the way they do, we must travel back tens of thousands of years to the environments in which human instincts were honed. Our ancestors were hunter-gatherers, living in small, tightly-knit communities where survival depended on making rapid, high-stakes decisions under uncertainty. The behaviors that increased chances of survival identifying threats, securing resources, and coordinating socially were reinforced over generations. Today, these same instincts manifest in financial markets as predictable cognitive and emotional biases.

From Survival to Speculation

Consider the environment of early humans:

- **Scarcity and risk sensitivity:** Food, water, and shelter were limited. A poor decision could result in immediate loss of life. Humans evolved to be extremely cautious with losses and highly attentive to potential threats.
- **Pattern recognition:** Survival required detecting subtle patterns in nature tracking animal movements, weather changes, and environmental cues. This predisposition for pattern recognition persists in traders' tendency to see trends, cycles, and correlations in markets.
- **Social influence:** Cooperation and observation of others' behavior ensured group survival. Modern traders inherit this instinct as herd behavior, social proof, and the compulsion to follow the crowd.

The market is, in essence, a simulated survival environment. Profits and losses substitute for resources, but the psychological machinery remains the same. Decisions are made under uncertainty, risk is omnipresent, and social influence is powerful just like in the savannah.

The Biases Born from Ancient Instincts

These instincts, while adaptive in the ancestral environment, create systematic biases in modern markets:

- **Loss aversion:** The fear of losing resources was critical for survival. Today, it manifests as holding onto losing positions too long or avoiding risk even when the potential reward is favorable.
- **Overreaction to novelty:** Our ancestors' attention to new threats ensured survival. In markets, this translates to exaggerated reactions to news, rumors, or unexpected events.
- **Herding behavior:** Following the group increased chances of survival. In trading, this emerges as FOMO, momentum chasing, and over-leveraging during bubbles.
- **Short-term focus:** Immediate threats mattered more than long-term gains in prehistoric life. This predisposes traders to impatience, impulsivity, and neglect of long-term strategy.

Why Biases Persist

These biases persist because they are rooted in neural circuits designed to maximize survival, not profits. Dopamine, cortisol, and other neurotransmitters reward rapid, instinctive responses. The market, with its highs, lows, wins, and losses, taps into the same reward and fear pathways that guided our ancestors. Even the most sophisticated trader is not immune; awareness and structured strategy are required to counteract these deep-seated tendencies.

From Instinct to Strategic Advantage

Understanding the evolutionary origins of trading biases is not just academic it is practical. By recognizing which instincts are influencing your decisions:

- You can distinguish genuine market signals from emotional noise.
- You can design systems and rules to counteract impulsive reactions.
- You can anticipate common crowd behaviors, exploiting predictable patterns created by shared instincts.

Markets are essentially a stage on which ancient instincts play out in modern forms. Every panic sell, euphoric rally, and hesitant consolidation is the reflection of tens of thousands of years of survival wiring. Traders who comprehend these dynamics gain an edge not just by reading charts, but by reading the minds and instincts of the crowd itself.

Key Insight

> *Our brains were wired to survive, not to trade. Recognizing how hunter-gatherer instincts manifest as trading biases allows us to anticipate crowd behavior and make decisions that leverage our evolutionary wiring rather than fall victim to it.*

4.2 Loss Aversion and Survival Wiring

Among all the instincts inherited from our hunter-gatherer ancestors, one stands out as the most powerful in shaping financial behavior: the fear of loss. Loss aversion the tendency to weigh potential losses more heavily than equivalent gains is deeply embedded in the human brain. It evolved as a survival mechanism: in environments where resources were scarce and mistakes could be fatal, avoiding losses often mattered more than seeking gains. In markets, this wiring creates predictable behavioral patterns, influencing both individual traders and entire crowds.

The Neuroscience Behind Loss Aversion

Research in behavioral economics and neuroscience reveals that losses activate stronger emotional responses than gains. The amygdala, a key region involved in threat detection, becomes highly active when facing potential losses, triggering stress, fear, and avoidance behaviors. Dopamine, associated with reward and motivation, responds asymmetrically: gains feel good, but losses feel much worse often two to three times more intensely. This asymmetry explains why traders panic-sell losing positions while failing to take profits consistently on winners.

Manifestations in Trading Behavior

Loss aversion impacts trading in several ways:

- **Holding losers too long:** Traders cling to losing positions, hoping for a rebound to avoid realizing a loss, often violating risk management rules.
- **Premature selling of winners:** Profitable positions are closed too early to "lock in gains," preventing the full potential of trends.
- **Overreaction to drawdowns:** Minor setbacks are perceived as catastrophic, prompting impulsive decisions and increased volatility in behavior.
- **Underestimation of risk-adjusted opportunity:** Fear of potential loss can prevent traders from taking asymmetric setups with favorable odds.

Crowd-Level Implications

On a collective scale, loss aversion amplifies market swings:

- During downturns, fear spreads rapidly, leading to panic selling and exaggerated price declines.
- In rallies, the avoidance of missing out creates herd behavior and momentum chasing.
- Market tops and bottoms are often driven more by collective emotional response than by fundamentals.

Strategies to Mitigate Loss Aversion

Awareness of survival wiring is the first step to managing its influence:

- **Define risk explicitly:** Use position sizing and stop-loss levels based on calculated risk, not emotion.

- **Focus on probabilities, not outcomes:** Emphasize expected value rather than individual wins or losses.
- **Maintain a trading journal:** Document emotional reactions to losses to identify patterns and biases.
- **Normalize small losses:** Accept that losses are part of trading; treating them as learning opportunities reduces emotional stress.

Evolutionary Perspective: Why This Wiring Exists

From an evolutionary standpoint, loss aversion was essential. A hunter who risked too much might die or lose scarce food, while one who avoided losses survived longer and passed on genes. In modern markets, the stakes are different, but the wiring remains. Recognizing this allows traders to consciously counterbalance instinct with strategy, turning a primal bias into an opportunity for disciplined advantage.

Key Insight

> *Loss aversion is hardwired for survival, not trading success. By understanding how this instinct shapes decisions, traders can structure strategies to act rationally, manage risk, and exploit opportunities that the crowd may avoid due to fear.*

4.3 Dopamine, Anticipation, and Reward Loops

Financial markets are not just numbers and charts they are a playground for the human brain's reward system. At the heart of many trading behaviors lies dopamine, a neurotransmitter that regulates motivation, pleasure, and learning. Dopamine is less about the reward itself and more about the anticipation of reward. This distinction is crucial: traders are often driven by the thrill of potential gains rather than the gains themselves, creating behavioral loops that can both fuel success and trigger destructive patterns.

The Role of Dopamine in Trading

Dopamine spikes in response to anticipated rewards, activating circuits in the brain that increase attention, motivation, and action. In trading:

- **Anticipation of profit:** Even the possibility of a successful trade can trigger dopamine release, increasing excitement and focus.
- **Near misses and partial gains:** "Almost winning" situations amplify dopamine activity, reinforcing risk-taking and engagement.

- **Novelty and surprise:** Unexpected price movements or opportunities stimulate dopamine, often leading traders to overreact or chase patterns.

The thrill of anticipation can be addictive. Traders often chase setups not purely based on analysis, but because the potential reward triggers the same neurochemical response as other pleasurable experiences creating cycles of craving, action, and reinforcement.

Reward Loops and Behavioral Biases

Dopamine-driven reward loops can explain several common trading behaviors:

- **Overtrading:** Seeking the excitement of potential gains rather than waiting for high-probability setups.
- **Chasing trends:** Entering positions late because the market's movement stimulates the anticipation of reward.
- **Ignoring risk:** Dopamine can temporarily overshadow rational evaluation, leading to underestimation of losses or leverage risk.
- **Reinforcement of patterns:** Successes create a positive feedback loop, making traders more confident and sometimes overconfident in repeated behaviors.

These loops are natural consequences of how our brains evolved. In ancestral environments, taking calculated risks could result in food, mates, or status. Today, the "rewards" are profits, recognition, or validation, but the neurochemical responses are identical.

Anticipation vs. Outcome

Interestingly, dopamine responds more strongly to the anticipation of reward than to the reward itself. This is why traders often feel the most excitement during trade entry or while a position is running, rather than after taking profits. Understanding this distinction helps explain why the act of trading can feel addictive and why emotions often peak before outcomes are realized.

Practical Implications for Traders

To harness dopamine loops effectively:

- **Awareness of emotional triggers:** Recognize when excitement is driving decisions rather than rational analysis.
- **Structured trading rules:** Let systematic criteria dictate entries and exits, preventing impulsive, dopamine-driven actions.

- **Reflection and journaling:** Track emotional highs and lows to identify patterns in impulsive or overconfident behavior.
- **Mindful engagement:** Use techniques like meditation or pause routines to reduce the dominance of anticipation-driven impulses.

Evolutionary Perspective

From an evolutionary standpoint, dopamine-driven risk-taking increased chances of acquiring resources and reproductive success. Our brains are wired to seek opportunity, take calculated risks, and repeat behaviors that yielded rewards. In markets, this wiring manifests as both opportunity and danger enabling disciplined traders to capitalize on patterns, but leading impulsive traders into overexposure and emotional mistakes.

Key Insight

> *Dopamine makes anticipation more powerful than outcome. By understanding its influence, traders can recognize when excitement is clouding judgment, use it to their advantage, and avoid being trapped in reward loops that lead to impulsive or destructive behavior.*

4.4 Actionable Insight: Observe Your Own Instincts During Trades

Understanding the evolutionary origins of trading behavior loss aversion, dopamine-driven reward loops, and survival wiring is only valuable if applied consciously. The final step in this chapter is self-observation: turning knowledge of human nature into a practical tool for improving trading decisions. By systematically monitoring your instincts and emotional responses, you can identify recurring patterns, reduce impulsivity, and gain a significant edge.

Why Observation Matters

Every trader experiences repeated emotional responses fear, excitement, regret, overconfidence but few track them consistently. Left unchecked, these reactions shape decisions subconsciously, often leading to predictable mistakes. Observing your instincts allows you to:

- Separate rational analysis from emotional impulses.
- Recognize when evolutionary biases are influencing judgment.
- Adjust strategies to exploit predictable patterns rather than fall victim to them.

Practical Methods for Observation

1. Maintain a Trading Journal: Record each trade with not only technical details (entry, exit, size, setup) but also emotional context:

- What emotions did you feel before entering?
- Were you acting on fear, hope, greed, or anticipation?
- Did dopamine-driven excitement influence your decision?

2. Identify Recurring Emotional Patterns: After several weeks, review your journal to identify repeated behaviors. For example:

- Do you consistently hold losing positions too long due to fear of loss?
- Do you enter trades impulsively when excitement peaks?
- Are there predictable times when regret or FOMO drives your decisions?

3. Implement Pause and Reflection Techniques: Before executing trades, pause to ask:

- Am I reacting to a market signal or an emotional impulse?
- Which instinct fear, greed, survival wiring is influencing me right now?
- Am I following my rules or chasing dopamine-driven excitement?

4. Create Behavioral Checklists: Develop a personal checklist for entries and exits that includes emotional self-assessment. This externalizes impulse control and ensures decisions align with strategy rather than instinct alone.

Leveraging Insights for Strategic Advantage

Observing and understanding your instincts transforms evolutionary wiring from a liability into an asset:

- **Anticipate crowd behavior:** Your own emotional patterns often mirror the market's. Recognizing them gives clues about collective psychology.
- **Enhance discipline:** Awareness reduces impulsivity and strengthens adherence to high-probability setups.
- **Develop emotional resilience:** Regular self-reflection diminishes the power of fear, greed, and overexcitement over time.

Actionable Exercise

1. Keep a detailed journal of all trades for at least 30 days, emphasizing emotional responses.
2. At the end of each week, highlight recurring patterns both positive and negative.
3. Adjust your trading rules or risk management strategies based on these observations.
4. Repeat the cycle, using your instincts as a guide rather than a constraint.

Key Insight

Your instincts are the echo of tens of thousands of years of evolution. Observing and understanding them allows you to turn primal wiring into a strategic advantage, mastering both your own behavior and, by extension, the collective behavior of the market.

Part II

The Psychology of Money And Markets

Chapter 5

Fear: The Market's Most Powerful Force

Fear is the most primal and pervasive emotion in financial markets. It moves faster than reason, spreads quicker than news, and shapes decisions in ways that often defy logic. Panic selling, herd retreats, and sudden market crashes are all manifestations of collective fear, reflecting deep-seated survival instincts that have been embedded in human psychology for millennia.

This chapter explores how fear influences both individual traders and entire markets. We will examine the mechanisms through which fear distorts perception of risk and time, creating irrational behaviors and emotional contagion. More importantly, we will provide practical techniques to reframe fear, transforming it from a paralyzing force into a tool for alertness, disciplined decision-making, and strategic advantage.

5.1 Panic Selling, Herd Retreats, and Emotional Contagion

Fear is contagious. In financial markets, individual anxiety rarely remains isolated; it spreads through traders, investors, and institutions, creating waves of collective behavior that can overwhelm rational analysis. Panic selling, herd retreats, and emotional contagion are the most visible manifestations of this phenomenon, often resulting in sharp declines, volatility spikes, and market dislocations.

Panic Selling: The Immediate Emotional Response

Panic selling occurs when fear triggers immediate, emotionally-driven decisions to exit positions, often at unfavorable prices. This behavior is rooted in survival instincts: just as early humans fled perceived threats to avoid danger, traders sell to escape potential losses even if fundamentals remain intact.

- **Signs in the market:** Sudden volume surges, sharp price declines, widening bid-ask spreads, and spikes in volatility indices.
- **Trader behavior:** Emotional urgency, abandoning strategy, and reacting to perceived threats rather than analysis.
- **Implication:** While panic selling may temporarily suppress prices, it often creates opportunities for disciplined traders who recognize that fear, not fundamentals, is driving the move.

Herd Retreats: Collective Amplification of Fear

Fear rarely acts in isolation. Humans are wired to observe and emulate the behavior of others, particularly in uncertain situations. Herd retreats occur when individuals collectively follow the crowd, amplifying downward movements or reinforcing extreme positions.

- **Mechanism:** Social proof and the avoidance of standing out push traders to mimic the majority.
- **Impact:** Herding can magnify losses, accelerate declines, and transform localized selling into market-wide panic.
- **Historical examples:** The 1929 stock market crash, the 1987 Black Monday, and the 2008 financial crisis all saw herd retreats exacerbating the downward spiral.

Emotional Contagion: Fear Spreads Faster Than Reason

Fear spreads not just through observation but through subtle psychological signals news headlines, social media chatter, market commentary, and even body language in trading rooms. Emotional contagion ensures that fear becomes self-reinforcing, often triggering disproportionate reactions.

- **Channels of contagion:** Media amplification, investor networks, online forums, and institutional signaling.
- **Effects on markets:** Heightened volatility, sudden liquidity withdrawal, and feedback loops where fear begets more fear.
- **Trader awareness:** Recognizing contagion helps distinguish genuine market signals from mass emotional reactions.

Why Fear is Not Always Negative

While fear can create chaos, it also serves as a signal:

- Extreme fear often precedes market bottoms and buying opportunities.
- Awareness of herd behavior allows disciplined traders to act contrarian, exploiting temporary mispricings.
- Fear highlights areas of high risk and emotional exposure, guiding position sizing and risk management decisions.

Actionable Takeaways

- Observe volume and volatility spikes as indicators of panic-driven activity.
- Compare price action with fundamentals to identify when fear, rather than information, is driving decisions.
- Maintain emotional distance: pause before acting, review your strategy, and avoid reacting to herd behavior.
- Use historical patterns of fear and panic as reference points for contrarian opportunities.

Key Insight

> *Fear is the invisible hand that moves markets, often faster than reason can react. By recognizing panic selling, herd retreats, and emotional contagion, traders can anticipate extreme behaviors, manage their own responses, and transform fear from a threat into a strategic advantage.*

5.2 How Fear Distorts Time Perception and Risk Judgment

Fear does more than trigger immediate reactions it fundamentally alters how traders perceive time, risk, and probability. When fear is heightened, the brain prioritizes survival over rational calculation, skewing judgment and leading to decisions that often magnify losses or cause missed opportunities. Understanding these distortions is critical for managing emotional responses and improving trading outcomes.

Time Perception Under Fear

Fear compresses subjective time, creating a sense of urgency that is often disproportionate to the actual risk. Traders may feel that a price drop is occurring faster than it actually is, leading to hasty exits or overreactions.

- **Hyperfocus on short-term movements:** Fear narrows attention to immediate threats, causing traders to overlook long-term trends or fundamental context.
- **Impatience and impulsivity:** Perceived "lost time" triggers rapid decisions, often without proper analysis or adherence to trading rules.
- **Perception of acceleration:** Minor price declines feel catastrophic, while minor rallies feel fleeting, distorting risk-reward evaluation.

Risk Perception Under Fear

Fear amplifies the perceived severity of potential losses and underestimates the likelihood of favorable outcomes. This cognitive distortion leads to risk-averse or panic-driven behavior, regardless of actual probabilities.

- **Overestimation of loss:** The emotional impact of a potential loss feels larger than the statistical risk, causing hesitation or avoidance.
- **Underestimation of opportunity:** Fear suppresses recognition of high-probability setups, making traders miss profitable trades.
- **Imbalanced decision-making:** Risk-reward calculations become skewed by emotional weight rather than objective analysis.

Neuroscience of Fear and Decision-Making

Fear activates the amygdala, which overrides the prefrontal cortex the region responsible for rational thought, planning, and self-control. This "amygdala hijack" is why traders act impulsively during crises, often violating their own strategies.

- Emotional responses dominate analytical thinking.
- Cortisol spikes impair memory and focus, reducing the ability to recall successful past strategies.
- Dopamine and adrenaline interact, producing heightened arousal that can lead to overtrading or aggressive exits.

Practical Implications for Traders

Understanding how fear distorts perception allows traders to implement strategies that maintain rational decision-making:

- **Predefine risk:** Set stop-loss levels and position sizes before entering trades to reduce fear-driven adjustments.
- **Use objective metrics:** Rely on technical, fundamental, or probabilistic frameworks to counteract subjective distortions.
- **Pause and assess:** When fear spikes, take a moment to review market context and confirm whether actions align with strategy.
- **Mindfulness and reflection:** Track emotional states in a trading journal to recognize patterns of distorted perception and improve future responses.

Key Insight

> *Fear warps both time and risk perception, making threats appear larger and opportunities smaller than they truly are. By recognizing these distortions, traders can detach from immediate emotional reactions, restore rational judgment, and make decisions that are aligned with strategy rather than instinct.*

5.3 Techniques to Reframe Fear into Alertness

Fear, when understood and managed, need not be a liability in trading. Instead of allowing fear to trigger impulsive reactions, traders can reframe it as a signal a source of heightened awareness, focus, and disciplined action. This section explores practical techniques to convert fear from a paralyzing emotion into a tool for alert, strategic decision-making.

1. Awareness and Labeling

The first step in reframing fear is recognition. By consciously identifying the emotion, traders prevent automatic, unconscious reactions.

- Pause and ask: "Am I feeling fear right now? What specifically am I afraid of?"
- Name the fear: labeling the emotion ("fear of loss," "fear of missing out") reduces its intensity by activating prefrontal reasoning.
- Track emotional triggers in a journal to identify recurring patterns and refine strategies.

2. Cognitive Reframing

Cognitive reframing shifts perception from threat to opportunity. Fear is a natural alert system by interpreting it as information rather than danger, traders can act thoughtfully.

- Reframe market volatility as potential setups rather than threats.
- Ask: "What does this fear tell me about the market and the crowd?"
- Recognize that fear-driven extremes often create asymmetric trading opportunities, where disciplined action yields outsized advantage.

3. Controlled Exposure and Gradual Desensitization

Repeated, conscious exposure to fear-inducing situations in a controlled manner builds resilience.

- Simulate stressful trading scenarios in paper trading or small positions.
- Gradually increase exposure to higher-risk trades while monitoring emotional responses.
- Over time, the same market conditions will trigger less panic, allowing rational decision-making under pressure.

4. Breathing, Mindfulness, and Body Awareness

Fear is both psychological and physiological. Techniques that calm the body can modulate the emotional response.

- Deep diaphragmatic breathing to reduce cortisol spikes.
- Mindfulness meditation to observe fear without reacting.
- Body scanning to notice tension, heartbeat, or muscle tightness signals that fear is influencing decision-making.

5. Checklists and Rule-Based Strategies

Fear often causes deviation from strategy. Externalizing decision-making reduces the influence of emotion.

- Create pre-defined entry, exit, and risk rules.
- Use checklists to confirm trades align with strategy before acting.
- Include emotional self-assessment as a step: only proceed if fear is acknowledged and accounted for.

6. Perspective Shifts

Broadening perspective diminishes the overwhelming immediacy of fear.

- Evaluate positions in the context of long-term strategy rather than moment-to-moment fluctuations.
- Recognize that market extremes are cyclical and temporary.
- View fear as a universal experience both your own and that of the crowd which can help identify potential contrarian opportunities.

7. Reflection and Learning

Post-trade reflection consolidates learning and strengthens future responses.

- Record emotional state, decisions, and outcomes.
- Identify whether fear led to premature exits, overtrading, or missed opportunities.
- Adjust rules, mental exercises, or exposure techniques based on insights.

Key Insight

Fear is not the enemy it is a signal. By observing, reframing, and channeling fear into alertness, traders transform a primal emotional response into a strategic advantage, gaining clarity, focus, and the ability to act decisively when others panic.

Chapter 6

Greed: The Hidden Addiction

While fear drives market sell-offs, greed often fuels the opposite extreme unchecked risk-taking, overexposure, and the pursuit of ever-larger gains. Greed is not merely a moral failing or character flaw; it is a deeply rooted psychological and neurobiological force. The same reward circuits that respond to food, social validation, or addictive substances are triggered by profits, creating a potent drive that can overwhelm rational analysis.

This chapter explores how greed manifests in trading and investing, why it often drives repeated behavioral mistakes, and how it contributes to the formation of market tops and speculative bubbles. We will examine the psychological mechanisms underlying the "next big win" mentality, the cyclical nature of greed-driven markets, and strategies for recognizing and managing this hidden addiction.

By understanding greed as a natural, predictable force, traders can anticipate its influence not only within themselves but across the broader market turning awareness into disciplined opportunity rather than uncontrolled risk.

6.1 Why Profits Stimulate the Same Circuits as Drugs

The human brain is wired to seek rewards, and financial gains activate the same neural pathways associated with pleasure, motivation, and addiction. When a trader makes a profit, the brain releases dopamine a neurotransmitter that signals reward and reinforces behavior. This is the same chemical system that responds to food, sex, or addictive substances, making profits inherently stimulating and, in some cases, habit-forming.

The Neurobiology of Profit

- **Dopamine spikes:** Each successful trade triggers dopamine release, creating a sensation of pleasure and reinforcing the behaviors that led to the gain.
- **Anticipatory excitement:** Just as with addictive substances, the anticipation of profit often produces more dopamine than the actual gain itself. This drives traders to seek the "next hit," fostering repeated risk-taking.
- **Reward prediction errors:** When gains exceed expectations, dopamine surges, reinforcing risk-seeking behavior. Conversely, unexpected losses suppress dopamine, producing discomfort and motivating corrective action, often in emotionally reactive ways.

Behavioral Consequences in Trading

The neurochemical rewards of profits have profound effects on behavior:

- **Chasing gains:** Traders may enter positions impulsively, seeking to replicate prior successes.
- **Overconfidence:** Frequent wins can inflate self-perception, leading to riskier decisions.
- **Addiction cycles:** Like substance use, the brain craves repeated stimulation, which can result in overtrading or compulsive behavior.
- **Ignoring risk:** Dopamine-driven reward can overshadow objective assessment of downside, increasing vulnerability to losses.

Historical and Market Examples

Market phenomena such as the Dot-com bubble, cryptocurrency frenzies, and rapid speculative rallies illustrate how collective greed, fueled by dopamine-driven excitement, can escalate asset prices beyond fundamental values. Individual traders within these cycles often experience intense emotional highs as profits accumulate, reinforcing the desire for larger and faster gains.

Practical Implications for Traders

- Recognize that the pleasure of profits is biologically reinforced self-awareness is the first defense.
- Establish rules-based strategies to limit impulsive risk-taking and overtrading.
- Track emotional highs in a trading journal to identify patterns of dopamine-driven decisions.

- Balance reward-seeking behavior with disciplined risk management to prevent destructive cycles.

Key Insight

Profits are biologically addictive. Understanding that your brain reacts to gains like it does to other rewards allows you to manage greed consciously, harness it strategically, and avoid falling into cycles of overconfidence and impulsive risk.

6.2 The Danger of the "Next Big Win" Mentality

One of the most insidious effects of greed in trading is the constant pursuit of the "next big win." This mentality driven by the dopamine-fueled pleasure of past successes creates a cycle of escalating risk-taking, overconfidence, and emotional volatility. Traders often believe that replicating prior wins is easy, underestimating the role of probability, market context, and chance.

Psychological Mechanisms Behind the Next Big Win

- **Recency Bias:** Recent successes loom large in memory, making past wins seem more predictive of future outcomes than they are. Traders may overestimate their skill based on short-term performance.
- **Variable Reward Schedules:** Like gambling, markets provide intermittent reinforcement occasional large wins amidst smaller or neutral outcomes which strengthens compulsive pursuit of the next opportunity.
- **Overconfidence and Illusion of Control:** Frequent wins inflate self-perception, making traders believe they can predict market movements, even when randomness is a major factor.
- **FOMO and Social Comparison:** Observing peers achieve significant gains intensifies the pressure to outperform, reinforcing the desire for quick, large profits.

Behavioral Consequences in Trading

The pursuit of the next big win manifests in several high-risk behaviors:

- **Overleveraging:** Traders increase position size to capture outsized gains, ignoring risk management rules.
- **Chasing trends:** Entry decisions are driven by the fear of missing out, rather than a systematic strategy.

- **Impatience:** Patience for high-probability setups declines, replaced by impulsive decisions in search of rapid profits.
- **Emotional volatility:** Wins produce euphoric highs, while minor losses trigger disproportionate frustration or panic, destabilizing decision-making.

Market Implications

When many participants fall prey to the "next big win" mentality, it creates self-reinforcing cycles:

- **Asset bubbles:** Herding toward high-return opportunities drives prices beyond fundamental values.
- **Increased volatility:** Rapid inflows and outflows amplify price swings.
- **Market tops and crashes:** Collective greed peaks just before corrections, as euphoria transitions into fear and panic.

Strategies to Counter the Next Big Win Trap

- **Rule-based trading:** Predefined entries, exits, and risk limits reduce emotional impulses.
- **Focus on process, not outcome:** Prioritize adherence to strategy over chasing profits.
- **Reflect on past behavior:** Maintain a trading journal to identify compulsive pursuit patterns.
- **Mindful awareness:** Pause and question whether trades are motivated by analysis or the lure of a quick win.

Key Insight

> *The pursuit of the "next big win" is a trap fueled by biology and psychology. Recognizing it allows traders to shift focus from fleeting victories to disciplined, process-driven decision-making turning greed from a destructive force into a measured tool for consistent success.*

6.3 Greed Cycles and Market Tops

Greed is not a constant it flows in cycles, waxing and waning with market conditions, news, and collective sentiment. These cycles often drive asset bubbles, speculative manias, and ultimately market tops, where valuations disconnect dramatically from fundamentals. Understanding how greed evolves collectively allows traders and investors to anticipate extremes and act with strategic discipline.

The Anatomy of a Greed Cycle

Greed cycles often follow predictable emotional and behavioral stages:

1. **Early Accumulation:** Smart money begins positioning quietly. Market activity is rational and opportunities are relatively low-risk.
2. **Rising Optimism:** Prices increase steadily. Traders notice gains and begin entering positions, driven by positive reinforcement from early successes.
3. **Euphoria:** Greed peaks as asset prices surge. Media hype, social proof, and stories of rapid wealth create mass participation. Rational evaluation often diminishes.
4. **Excess and Overconfidence:** Risk is underestimated, leverage increases, and the "next big win" mentality dominates. Traders feel invincible.
5. **Market Top:** Collective greed reaches its apex. Liquidity dries up, selling pressure from early movers begins, and even minor negative news can trigger a reversal.

Behavioral Drivers of Market Tops

Several psychological mechanisms underpin these cycles:

- **Herd behavior:** As more participants chase gains, individual rationality is overridden by the fear of missing out.
- **Confirmation bias:** Traders selectively focus on information that supports their bullish narrative, ignoring warning signs.
- **Overconfidence and illusion of control:** Repeated wins inflate perceived skill, leading to reckless decisions.
- **Social proof and media amplification:** News, influencers, and peer stories reinforce the sense that the trend will continue indefinitely.

Historical Examples

Market history provides clear illustrations of greed-driven peaks:

- **Tulip Mania (1637):** Speculative frenzy drove tulip bulb prices to extraordinary levels, detached from intrinsic value.

- **Dot-com Bubble (1999–2000):** Tech stocks soared as optimism and greed overshadowed fundamental valuations.
- **Cryptocurrency Mania (2017, 2021):** Rapid adoption and media hype fueled euphoric buying, followed by sharp corrections.

Practical Implications for Traders

Understanding greed cycles allows for strategic positioning:

- Recognize the stage of the cycle before increasing exposure euphoria and excess signal heightened risk.
- Avoid being the last entrant into a crowded trade; late participation often leads to losses.
- Monitor sentiment indicators, market narratives, and unusual price behavior to anticipate turning points.
- Combine behavioral insights with technical and fundamental analysis to identify asymmetric risk-reward opportunities.

Actionable Takeaways

- Maintain discipline during bullish extremes; resist the pressure of herd behavior.
- Document market behavior and your own emotional responses to identify recurring greed patterns.
- Use greed cycles as a contrarian indicator peaks in collective optimism often precede corrections.

Key Insight

Greed drives markets to irrational extremes, creating cycles that culminate in tops and bubbles. By understanding these psychological patterns, traders can anticipate turning points, manage risk, and act strategically while others are blinded by the lure of profits.

Chapter 7

Ego and Overconfidence

While fear and greed drive much of market behavior, ego and overconfidence subtly influence decisions in ways that are often overlooked. Traders frequently confuse luck with skill, attributing random successes to personal mastery rather than chance. This misperception fuels overconfidence, encourages excessive risk-taking, and reinforces the illusion of control over inherently uncertain markets.

In this chapter, we explore how ego shapes trading behavior, why overconfidence is one of the most persistent psychological pitfalls in finance, and how traders can build genuine confidence without letting ego compromise decision-making. By recognizing and managing these internal biases, you can maintain clarity, make disciplined choices, and prevent pride from undermining long-term performance.

7.1 Why Traders Confuse Luck with Skill

In financial markets, success is often a mixture of skill, strategy, and chance. However, human psychology has a strong tendency to overattribute outcomes to personal ability while underestimating the role of randomness. This misattribution fosters overconfidence, encourages excessive risk-taking, and creates a distorted perception of control.

The Role of Randomness in Trading

Markets are inherently probabilistic. Even well-researched trades can fail, and poorly timed decisions can occasionally succeed. Traders who experience repeated positive outcomes may erroneously assume that their skill is the primary driver, ignoring the significant influence of chance.

- **Survivorship bias:** Successful traders often focus on their wins while overlooking losses, reinforcing the belief in their own skill.

- **Recency bias:** Recent successes loom larger in memory, leading traders to overestimate their predictive abilities.
- **Confirmation bias:** Traders selectively notice information that supports their perceived competence, dismissing contradictory evidence.

Psychological Mechanisms Behind Misattribution

Several cognitive processes contribute to confusing luck with skill:

- **Illusion of control:** Humans tend to believe they can influence outcomes in situations governed largely by chance.
- **Pattern recognition bias:** The brain seeks meaningful patterns, sometimes finding order where none exists, leading traders to believe they predicted a move correctly.
- **Emotional reinforcement:** Positive outcomes trigger dopamine release, creating pleasurable feedback loops that strengthen the perception of skill.

Behavioral Consequences in Trading

Misattributing luck to skill can have serious implications:

- **Overtrading:** Confidence from lucky wins leads to taking excessive positions or increasing trade frequency.
- **Neglecting risk management:** Belief in personal invincibility reduces adherence to stop-losses, position sizing rules, and hedging strategies.
- **Ignoring learning opportunities:** Traders fail to analyze mistakes or understand the role of randomness, slowing skill development.

Practical Strategies to Counter Misattribution

- Keep a detailed trading journal to separate skill-driven decisions from luck-driven outcomes.
- Conduct post-trade analysis to evaluate whether results align with strategy or chance.
- Study statistical probabilities and market behavior to contextualize wins and losses.
- Maintain humility: recognize that every trader experiences luck and that overconfidence can be costly.

Key Insight

Confusing luck with skill is a natural cognitive bias, but awareness and disciplined reflection can prevent it from undermining long-term success. By distinguishing between randomness and competence, traders cultivate realistic confidence and make decisions grounded in analysis rather than ego.

7.2 The Illusion of Control

One of the most subtle and dangerous cognitive biases in trading is the illusion of control the belief that we can influence or predict outcomes in inherently uncertain environments. This bias leads traders to overestimate their ability to steer results, underestimate risk, and act with unwarranted confidence. While feeling in control can be psychologically comforting, it often masks vulnerability to market randomness.

Psychological Roots of the Illusion of Control

Humans have evolved to seek patterns and causality in their environment. While this is adaptive in many contexts, it becomes maladaptive in probabilistic systems like financial markets.

- **Pattern-seeking:** The brain naturally looks for cause-and-effect relationships, even when outcomes are random.
- **Experience-based reinforcement:** Past successes, even when influenced by luck, reinforce the perception that actions directly caused positive results.
- **Desire for predictability:** Markets are uncertain, and humans are uncomfortable with randomness. Believing we have control reduces anxiety.

Manifestations in Trading Behavior

The illusion of control can influence traders in multiple ways:

- **Overleveraging:** Belief in personal skill leads to taking larger positions than risk parameters justify.
- **Excessive intervention:** Traders frequently adjust positions, believing they can "correct" outcomes that are largely unpredictable.
- **Confirmation-seeking:** Traders selectively focus on information that supports their perceived control, ignoring contrary signals.
- **Resistance to strategy:** Overconfidence in personal influence can override rules-based systems, resulting in impulsive decisions.

Consequences for Market Performance

Believing in control where none exists can amplify losses, create unnecessary stress, and hinder skill development:

- Increased emotional volatility when outcomes diverge from expectations.
- Reduced learning from failures, as losses are attributed to external "exceptions" rather than flawed assumptions or chance.
- Escalation of risk-taking, often culminating in avoidable drawdowns or catastrophic losses.

Strategies to Counter the Illusion of Control

- **Probabilistic thinking:** Approach each trade as a probability exercise rather than a guaranteed outcome.
- **Rules-based trading:** Adhere strictly to pre-defined entry, exit, and risk parameters to minimize ego-driven interference.
- **Post-trade analysis:** Evaluate whether results were influenced by skill, chance, or external factors.
- **Mindful self-assessment:** Pause before acting and ask: "Am I controlling this outcome, or is the market determining it?"
- **Accept uncertainty:** Embrace the inherent randomness of markets as a fundamental reality, not a flaw in your skill.

Key Insight

> *The illusion of control is a natural psychological bias, but in trading it can be costly. By recognizing the limits of personal influence, practicing probabilistic thinking, and relying on disciplined strategy, traders can make decisions grounded in reality rather than ego-driven illusion.*

7.3 Building Confidence Without Ego

Confidence is essential for trading success, but when it is intertwined with ego, it becomes dangerous. True trading confidence is grounded in skill, experience, and disciplined decision-making, rather than the emotional reinforcement of past wins or the desire to appear competent. This section explores how to cultivate authentic confidence while minimizing ego-driven pitfalls.

Differentiating Confidence from Ego

- **Confidence:** A realistic assessment of skills, knowledge, and ability to execute a strategy. It is flexible, humble, and informed by experience.
- **Ego:** An inflated sense of self-importance, often reinforced by external validation, luck, or past successes. Ego seeks recognition, dominance, or validation rather than optimal decision-making.
- **The danger of conflation:** When ego masquerades as confidence, traders take unnecessary risks, ignore evidence, and become blind to market realities.

Strategies to Build Authentic Confidence

- **Master the process, not the outcome:** Focus on executing your strategy correctly rather than obsessing over individual wins or losses. Consistent process mastery builds reliable confidence.
- **Incremental learning and reflection:** Regularly review trades, identify mistakes, and understand decision-making under various conditions. Experience grounded in analysis strengthens skill-based confidence.
- **Set realistic expectations:** Acknowledge market uncertainty and the probabilistic nature of outcomes. True confidence comes from preparation, not certainty of success.
- **Journaling and self-awareness:** Track emotional states, decisions, and results. Recognizing when ego influences choices allows you to adjust behavior proactively.
- **Focus on controllable factors:** Confidence grows when attention is given to aspects within your control, such as research, strategy, risk management, and execution, rather than trying to control market outcomes.

Behavioral Practices to Reinforce Confidence Without Ego

- **Mindfulness and emotional regulation:** Observe emotions without attachment, allowing rational decision-making to dominate over impulsive reactions.
- **Accountability partners or mentors:** Seeking feedback and guidance from experienced traders provides perspective and prevents ego inflation.

- **Simulated practice:** Paper trading or scenario simulations build confidence in executing strategies without the pressure of real financial stakes.
- **Celebrate learning, not just wins:** Rewarding skill development and disciplined decisions reinforces confidence independent of outcomes.

Key Insight

Confidence rooted in skill, preparation, and disciplined execution empowers traders to navigate markets effectively. By separating confidence from ego, you maintain clarity, make rational decisions under pressure, and cultivate long-term success without falling prey to overconfidence or hubris.

Chapter 8

Hope, Denial & Regret

Hope, denial, and regret are powerful emotional forces that influence how traders respond to losses and setbacks. While hope can motivate perseverance, unchecked it often leads to holding losing positions, falling into sunk-cost traps, or ignoring clear signals that a trade is failing. Denial magnifies these risks, preventing objective assessment of market realities. Meanwhile, regret can trigger impulsive behavior, including revenge trading, which further compounds losses.

In this chapter, we explore the psychological dynamics of these emotions, how they manifest in trading behavior, and practical strategies to manage them. You will learn how to accept losses without attachment, identify the cognitive biases that prolong mistakes, and transform regret into actionable insight. By mastering these emotional challenges, traders can cultivate resilience, maintain discipline, and convert painful experiences into a source of strategic advantage.

8.1 Holding Losers, Sunk-Cost Traps, Confirmation Bias

One of the most common and costly mistakes traders make is holding onto losing positions for too long. This behavior is often driven by emotional attachment, cognitive biases, and the psychological discomfort of admitting a mistake. Understanding the interplay between hope, denial, and regret is crucial for avoiding these traps.

The Sunk-Cost Trap

The sunk-cost trap occurs when traders continue investing time, capital, or effort into a losing trade simply because they have already committed resources. The logic is flawed: past losses are irrecoverable, and decisions should be based on the future probability of success rather than the desire to "make back" what was lost.

- **Emotional attachment:** Traders may view a losing position as a personal failure and hope that persistence will validate their original decision.
- **Escalating commitment:** The more one invests, the harder it becomes to exit, reinforcing the cycle of loss.
- **Ignoring rational signals:** Objective indicators, risk thresholds, or stop-loss rules are often overridden by emotional investment.

Confirmation Bias

Confirmation bias amplifies the sunk-cost trap by causing traders to selectively interpret information that supports their original belief while ignoring contradictory evidence. For example:

- Focusing on news, technical patterns, or opinions that justify holding a losing trade.
- Discounting signals that suggest the trade should be exited.
- Rationalizing losses as temporary setbacks rather than probabilistic outcomes.

Behavioral Consequences

The combination of sunk-cost thinking and confirmation bias leads to:

- **Excessive losses:** Positions are held far beyond reasonable risk thresholds.
- **Emotional distress:** Stress, anxiety, and regret intensify as losses grow.
- **Impaired decision-making:** Continued attachment clouds judgment, increasing the likelihood of further errors.

Practical Strategies to Avoid These Traps

- **Predefine exit rules:** Set stop-losses and profit targets before entering a trade to remove emotional interference.
- **Adopt probabilistic thinking:** Evaluate trades based on expected future outcomes, not past commitments.
- **Seek objective feedback:** Use mentors, peer review, or trading software to get an unbiased assessment of positions.

- **Reflect and journal:** Record emotional states, decision rationale, and outcomes to identify patterns of attachment and bias.

Key Insight

> *Holding onto losers is rarely rational; it is driven by hope, denial, and confirmation bias. Recognizing these psychological traps allows traders to act decisively, cut losses early, and convert emotional challenges into disciplined, data-driven decisions.*

8.2 How to Accept Pain Without Attachment

Loss and disappointment are inevitable aspects of trading and investing. Even the most disciplined traders will encounter losing trades, unexpected market moves, and periods of underperformance. The key to long-term success is not avoiding pain but learning to experience it without emotional overreaction or attachment to outcomes.

The Nature of Emotional Attachment

Attachment occurs when traders tie their self-worth, identity, or ego to market results. This creates several problems:

- **Amplified stress:** Losses feel personal, triggering anxiety, frustration, or anger.
- **Impaired decision-making:** Emotion-driven reactions override rational analysis and risk management.
- **Cycle of regret and revenge trading:** Emotional attachment to past losses can lead to impulsive attempts to "win it back."

Techniques for Emotional Detachment

- **Mindfulness and meditation:** Practice observing thoughts and emotions without judgment. This helps you acknowledge loss without reacting impulsively.
- **Cognitive reframing:** View losses as information and opportunities for learning, not as personal failure. Ask, "What can this teach me about strategy, timing, or risk management?"
- **Probabilistic mindset:** Focus on expected outcomes over individual trade results. Each trade is one of many in a larger statistical process.
- **Predefined risk parameters:** Accept loss limits as part of the plan. Knowing in advance how much you can lose reduces emotional volatility.

Journaling and Reflection

Documenting trades and emotional responses is essential:

- Record your rationale for each trade, the outcome, and your emotional state.
- Reflect on recurring patterns of attachment or overreaction.
- Use this insight to adjust strategies, improve discipline, and reduce emotional susceptibility.

Building Resilience Over Time

Repeated practice in detaching from outcomes strengthens emotional resilience:

- **Normalize losses:** Understand that losses are inherent in trading and are not a reflection of personal worth.
- **Focus on process mastery:** Shift attention from results to the quality of your decision-making. Process-driven confidence reduces attachment to outcomes.
- **Gradual exposure:** Start with small, controlled trades to practice detachment, then scale as emotional resilience grows.

Key Insight

Accepting pain without attachment transforms losses from emotional triggers into valuable feedback. By cultivating detachment, probabilistic thinking, and resilience, traders can navigate markets with clarity, reduce impulsive mistakes, and maintain consistent performance over the long term.

8.3 Revenge Trading Loops: Turning Regret Into Signal

Regret is one of the most powerful emotions in trading. It arises when traders feel they have missed an opportunity, exited too early, or taken a loss that could have been avoided. Left unchecked, regret often fuels revenge trading a cycle of impulsive, emotionally driven trades aimed at "making back" losses or missed gains. Understanding this cycle and learning to channel regret constructively can turn a potential liability into a strategic advantage.

The Mechanics of Revenge Trading

Revenge trading typically follows a predictable emotional and behavioral sequence:

1. **Trigger Event:** A loss, missed opportunity, or perceived mistake generates regret.
2. **Emotional Escalation:** Anxiety, frustration, and disappointment intensify, clouding judgment.
3. **Impulsive Action:** Traders enter new positions hastily, often with larger size or higher risk, hoping to "recover" prior losses.
4. **Compounding Mistakes:** These trades are frequently poorly planned, disregarding analysis or risk management, leading to additional losses.
5. **Reinforced Loop:** Each new loss strengthens emotional reactivity, creating a feedback loop that is difficult to break.

Psychological Drivers Behind Revenge Trading

Several cognitive biases and emotional triggers contribute to revenge trading:

- **Loss aversion:** Humans feel losses more acutely than equivalent gains, creating pressure to "recover" quickly.
- **Confirmation bias:** Traders selectively interpret information that justifies acting immediately, ignoring risk signals.
- **Recency bias:** Recent negative outcomes dominate perception, overshadowing long-term strategy or probabilistic reasoning.
- **Emotional contagion:** Observing others' success or market hype can intensify feelings of regret and urgency.

Transforming Regret Into Actionable Signal

Rather than reacting impulsively, regret can be leveraged as a signal for disciplined action:

- **Pause and assess:** Before taking any trade driven by regret, stop and evaluate the rationale. Ask: "Am I responding to market conditions or my emotions?"
- **Document lessons learned:** Maintain a regret journal to record missed opportunities, losses, and emotional triggers. Patterns reveal valuable insights.

- **Extract probabilistic signals:** Use regret as feedback on timing, strategy, or market conditions, rather than as a prompt to act impulsively.
- **Set corrective boundaries:** Define maximum trade sizes, risk limits, and waiting periods to prevent emotionally reactive decisions.

Behavioral Practices to Prevent Loops

- **Mindfulness techniques:** Observe emotional states without attachment or judgment, breaking automatic reaction chains.
- **Controlled reflection:** Review trades and regrets outside of active market hours to reduce emotional reactivity.
- **Scenario simulations:** Practice handling missed opportunities in paper trading or hypothetical setups to train response mechanisms.

Key Insight

Regret is an unavoidable part of trading, but it does not have to lead to destructive behavior. By recognizing revenge trading loops and using regret as a source of insight rather than impulse, traders can transform emotional discomfort into disciplined, strategic action that improves long-term performance.

Chapter 9

The Crowd Mind

Markets are not simply collections of individual traders; they are dynamic networks of interacting minds, influenced by collective psychology. The "crowd mind" refers to the aggregated behavior of market participants, where emotions, biases, and social dynamics combine to create predictable patterns. Understanding this collective mindset is essential for navigating price action, identifying opportunities, and avoiding the pitfalls of herd-driven decisions.

In this chapter, we explore the psychology behind herd behavior, the mechanisms of social proof, and how Fear of Missing Out (FOMO) functions as a modern expression of ancient tribal instincts. We will also examine the contrasting behaviors of smart money and retail participants, revealing how institutional strategies often exploit crowd tendencies. Finally, actionable insights will guide you in recognizing moments when the crowd's influence is strongest, helping you pause, reassess, and make rational, disciplined trading decisions.

9.1 Herd Behavior and Social Proof

Humans are inherently social creatures. From an evolutionary standpoint, following the group often increased survival odds, providing safety, shared resources, and collective knowledge. In financial markets, this same instinct manifests as herd behavior traders mimicking the actions of others, sometimes at the expense of rational analysis. Social proof, the psychological phenomenon where people assume the actions of others reflect correct behavior, reinforces this effect.

The Psychology Behind Herd Behavior

Herd behavior arises from several cognitive and emotional mechanisms:

- **Fear of isolation:** Traders often fear missing out or being wrong in isolation, prompting them to conform to the majority.

- **Information shortcut:** Observing what others are doing serves as a mental shortcut for decision-making, especially under uncertainty.
- **Validation seeking:** Following the crowd provides psychological reassurance, reducing anxiety about making independent judgments.

Social Proof in Market Contexts

Social proof amplifies herd behavior in financial markets. Examples include:

- **Momentum trading:** Traders buy assets simply because prices are rising and others are buying.
- **Media influence:** Headlines, analyst opinions, and social media can reinforce the perception that popular trades are correct.
- **Peer pressure:** Observing colleagues or respected figures taking positions can trigger mimicry.

Consequences of Herd Behavior

While collective behavior can create liquidity and trend momentum, it often leads to:

- **Overvaluation or bubbles:** Excessive buying due to herd enthusiasm drives prices beyond intrinsic value.
- **Panic selling:** Fear-driven mass exits amplify downturns and accelerate crashes.
- **Reduced critical thinking:** Conformity diminishes independent analysis and increases vulnerability to market manipulations.

Behavioral Strategies to Navigate Herd Influence

- **Pause and analyze:** Before following the crowd, ask whether the decision aligns with your strategy and risk parameters.
- **Quantitative assessment:** Evaluate market trends and indicators objectively rather than relying solely on social signals.
- **Maintain a contrarian mindset:** Recognize that crowded trades may offer asymmetric opportunities when approached strategically.
- **Track emotional triggers:** Notice when fear of missing out or desire for validation is influencing your decisions.

Key Insight

> *Herd behavior and social proof are powerful drivers of market dynamics. By understanding the psychological forces that compel collective action, traders can resist emotional contagion, identify real opportunities, and make decisions grounded in analysis rather than the whims of the crowd.*

9.2 FOMO as Modern Tribal Survival

Fear of Missing Out, commonly abbreviated as FOMO, is one of the most pervasive psychological drivers in modern markets. While it is often discussed casually in trading communities, its roots run deep in human evolution. For early humans, missing out on critical opportunities such as hunting, gathering, or forming alliances could have serious survival consequences. This same instinct persists today, subtly influencing traders' decisions and fueling herd behavior, speculative bubbles, and impulsive market actions.

The Evolutionary Origins of FOMO

FOMO is essentially a survival mechanism:

- **Resource competition:** In ancestral environments, failing to act on opportunities (food, shelter, mates) could threaten survival.
- **Social cohesion:** Aligning with group behavior strengthened protection and increased access to shared resources.
- **Status and reputation:** Early humans relied on social standing for support and cooperation; missing out on critical actions could damage social credibility.

In modern markets, the same wiring triggers emotional reactions when traders perceive an opportunity slipping away, even when the stakes are not existential.

Manifestations in Trading Behavior

FOMO manifests in several ways in financial markets:

- **Impulse buying:** Entering trades without analysis simply because others are profiting.
- **Chasing momentum:** Jumping into rising markets late, increasing exposure to risk and volatility.
- **Neglecting risk management:** Ignoring position sizing, stop-losses, or exit strategies in the pursuit of immediate gains.

- **Emotional amplification:** Social media, financial news, and peer discussions intensify feelings of urgency and fear of missing out.

The Cognitive Mechanisms Behind FOMO

Several psychological biases amplify FOMO:

- **Loss aversion:** Fear of missing profits feels like a loss relative to others' gains.
- **Social proof:** Observing peers' actions reinforces the notion that immediate participation is necessary.
- **Recency bias:** Recent success stories dominate perception, leading to an overestimation of opportunity probability.

Strategies to Manage FOMO

- **Develop a rules-based plan:** Predetermine entry, exit, and risk criteria to reduce emotional decisions.
- **Pause and evaluate:** Before acting, ask whether the decision is strategy-driven or fear-driven.
- **Focus on process over outcome:** Concentrate on disciplined execution rather than chasing short-term gains.
- **Awareness and journaling:** Record instances of FOMO to identify triggers, patterns, and areas for behavioral improvement.

Key Insight

> *FOMO is not a modern invention it is an ancient survival instinct misaligned with financial markets. Recognizing it, understanding its origins, and implementing disciplined strategies allows traders to convert instinctual impulses into measured, rational actions rather than reactive, high-risk decisions.*

9.3 Smart Money vs Dumb Money Psychology

Financial markets are arenas where two broad psychological archetypes often collide: the disciplined, informed behavior of institutional "smart money" and the reactive, emotion-driven behavior of retail or "dumb money." Understanding these contrasting mindsets is critical for identifying opportunities, avoiding common traps, and anticipating market movements.

Defining Smart Money and Dumb Money

- **Smart Money:** Typically refers to institutional investors, professional traders, hedge funds, and well-capitalized entities. They operate with:
  - Access to superior research and analytics.
  - Structured risk management and capital allocation strategies.
  - Patience, process-driven decision-making, and long-term perspective.
  - Psychological discipline, often using contrarian strategies to exploit crowd behavior.
- **Dumb Money:** Refers to individual or retail traders who often:
  - React impulsively to market news, hype, or social proof.
  - Chase trends and succumb to FOMO.
  - Lack systematic risk controls.
  - Confuse luck with skill, overreact to short-term outcomes, and are prone to emotional decision-making.

Psychological Drivers and Differences

- **Emotional Discipline:** Smart money operates with emotional detachment, following probabilistic strategies rather than impulse. Dumb money is influenced by fear, greed, regret, and hope.
- **Time Horizon:** Smart money can hold positions across market cycles, tolerating short-term pain for long-term gain. Dumb money often reacts to daily price swings, amplifying market volatility.
- **Information Processing:** Smart money interprets signals contextually, using data, sentiment analysis, and market structure. Dumb money reacts to headlines, peer opinions, and anecdotal evidence.
- **Herd Behavior:** Dumb money is more likely to participate in crowded trades, creating bubbles or panics. Smart money frequently anticipates and exploits these collective behaviors.

Behavioral Patterns in Practice

- **Accumulation and Distribution:** Smart money often accumulates positions quietly when retail participants are fearful and distributes (sells) when the crowd is euphoric.
- **Liquidity Hunting:** Smart money identifies clusters of stop-losses or emotional exit points of dumb money to enter or exit strategically.

- **Market Sentiment Exploitation:** By understanding retail biases like panic selling, FOMO buying, and confirmation bias smart money positions itself for asymmetric advantage.

Practical Insights for Traders

- **Observe Crowd Behavior:** Track market sentiment, volume spikes, and emotional extremes to anticipate potential reversals or continuation patterns.
- **Maintain Emotional Discipline:** Emulate smart money by prioritizing process, risk management, and probabilistic thinking over short-term excitement.
- **Use Contrarian Thinking:** Recognize that when the crowd is exuberant, caution may be warranted; when fear dominates, opportunities may arise.
- **Integrate Behavioral Awareness:** Document personal reactions and tendencies to avoid acting like the "dumb money" participant in emotionally charged environments.

Key Insight

> *Markets are shaped not just by fundamentals, but by the contrasting behaviors of smart and dumb money. By understanding these psychological dynamics, traders can align with informed, disciplined strategies, exploit collective biases, and navigate market cycles with greater precision and resilience.*

9.4 Actionable Insight: Track FOMO Moments Pause Trades and Ask if the Decision is Emotional or Rational

Fear of Missing Out (FOMO) is a subtle but powerful driver of poor trading decisions. Even experienced traders can fall prey to the urge to act impulsively when they see others profiting or when market momentum appears irresistible. The key to mastering the crowd mind is to transform these emotional impulses into moments of reflection and disciplined decision-making.

Recognizing FOMO Triggers

Before a trader can manage FOMO, it must first be recognized. Common triggers include:

- **Rapid price moves:** Sudden surges or drops can provoke the fear of missing opportunity or avoiding loss.
- **Social signals:** Discussions on forums, social media hype, or peer conversations suggesting a "must-act-now" opportunity.
- **Personal regret memory:** Previous missed gains or losses can prime a trader to react emotionally rather than strategically.

The Pause Principle

When a FOMO moment arises, the most effective tool is a deliberate pause:

- Step back from immediate action and breathe allow the emotional surge to subside.
- Ask structured questions:
  - "Am I entering this trade based on analysis or emotion?"
  - "Does this decision align with my risk parameters and trading plan?"
  - "Am I chasing the crowd or evaluating a genuine opportunity?"
- Use this pause to evaluate market data objectively rather than relying on instinctive reactions.

Tracking and Journaling FOMO Moments

Documenting emotional triggers creates long-term awareness:

- Maintain a **FOMO log**: Record instances when you felt compelled to act impulsively, noting the trigger, emotional intensity, and resulting action.
- Review patterns periodically to identify recurring biases or high-risk scenarios.
- Adjust strategies based on insights e.g., setting stricter rules for entering trades during high-volatility periods or crowded market conditions.

Transforming Emotion into Insight

Rather than eliminating emotion entirely, channel it constructively:

- Use FOMO as a **signal** that the market is experiencing crowd-driven behavior this may indicate opportunities for contrarian positioning or heightened caution.

- Analyze whether the emotional surge aligns with probabilistic market setups or is purely reactionary.
- Convert insights into actionable rules: limit trade size, implement pause protocols, or seek confirmation from objective indicators before acting.

Key Insight

FOMO is a natural response to market dynamics, but disciplined traders can transform it from a liability into a strategic tool. By pausing, reflecting, and tracking emotional impulses, you can make rational decisions, avoid herd-driven mistakes, and use crowd psychology to your advantage.

Part III

Behavioral Patterns & Market Cycles

Chapter 10

The Anatomy of a Market Cycle

Markets move in cycles, not purely because of economic data or fundamentals, but because of the collective emotions and behaviors of participants. Every rally, peak, decline, and recovery carries a distinct emotional signature, reflecting the hopes, fears, and decisions of individuals and institutions alike. Understanding these cycles is essential for anticipating market movements, managing risk, and positioning strategically.

In this chapter, we break down the typical phases of a market cycle Hope, Euphoria, Fear, Capitulation, and Recovery and explore the psychological forces driving each stage. We will examine why every boom and bust is fundamentally human rather than purely economic, how emotional patterns repeat across asset classes and eras, and how recognizing these signatures can help traders and investors navigate volatility with clarity. By studying the anatomy of cycles, readers can move from reactive participation to proactive insight, aligning their strategies with the underlying psychology of markets.

10.1 Hope → Euphoria → Fear → Capitulation → Recovery

Market cycles are essentially emotional waves, driven by the collective psychology of participants. While fundamentals provide context, it is human emotion that creates the rhythm of boom and bust. Each phase of the cycle carries distinct behaviors, sentiments, and opportunities for those who understand the underlying psychology.

1. Hope

Hope is the initial spark of a market cycle. Investors and traders sense opportunity, often after a period of stagnation or recovery from prior losses. This phase is characterized by cautious optimism:

- **Behavior:** Early accumulation of positions, selective participation, and moderate risk-taking.
- **Emotional signature:** Curiosity, anticipation, and tentative confidence.
- **Opportunity:** Strategic entry points exist for patient, disciplined participants who can distinguish genuine trends from false signals.

2. Euphoria

Euphoria represents the peak of collective optimism. Prices surge, narratives of limitless gains dominate, and fear of missing out drives mass participation. Emotional and behavioral traits include:

- **Behavior:** Aggressive buying, leveraging positions, ignoring risk management, chasing momentum.
- **Emotional signature:** Exuberance, overconfidence, and a sense of inevitability.
- **Risk:** Bubbles form as valuations detach from fundamentals, creating vulnerability to sharp reversals.

3. Fear

As the market peaks and early signs of decline appear, hope transforms into fear. Investors become anxious about potential losses:

- **Behavior:** Partial exits, hesitation to enter new trades, rising volatility.
- **Emotional signature:** Unease, doubt, and uncertainty.
- **Market impact:** Increased selling pressure can accelerate trend reversals, triggering short-term panic among less experienced participants.

4. Capitulation

Capitulation is the emotional nadir of the cycle, where fear reaches its peak and market participants surrender positions in a rush to avoid further losses:

- **Behavior:** Mass sell-offs, panic exits, disregard for fundamentals, often at extreme lows.

- **Emotional signature:** Desperation, regret, and helplessness.
- **Opportunity:** Contrarian investors and smart money often accumulate positions quietly, preparing for the next recovery phase.

5. Recovery

Following capitulation, the market slowly stabilizes as confidence begins to return. This phase sets the foundation for a new cycle:

- **Behavior:** Gradual buying, renewed interest from patient participants, and cautious optimism.
- **Emotional signature:** Relief, tentative hope, and renewed engagement.
- **Market impact:** Establishes the groundwork for the next cycle, often repeating familiar emotional patterns.

Key Insight

Market cycles are fundamentally emotional. By recognizing the Hope → Euphoria → Fear → Capitulation → Recovery sequence, traders and investors can anticipate behavioral extremes, position strategically, and navigate volatility with foresight rather than reaction. Understanding emotional signatures is as important if not more than analyzing charts or fundamentals.

10.2 Why Every Boom and Bust is Human, Not Economic

While economic data, corporate earnings, and interest rates provide context, the primary engine behind market booms and busts is human behavior. History shows that even when fundamentals are stable, collective psychology can drive prices far above or below intrinsic value. Understanding this principle is essential for traders and investors seeking to anticipate market extremes rather than react to them.

The Primacy of Emotion

Human emotions greed, fear, hope, and regret are deeply ingrained and often override rational calculation:

- **Greed:** Drives overvaluation during booms, as participants chase profits and ignore risk.

- **Fear:** Triggers panic selling during downturns, often exacerbating declines beyond what fundamentals justify.
- **Hope and denial:** Keep participants invested during early declines, delaying rational exits.

Even the most data-driven traders are susceptible to emotional contagion when a crowd reacts strongly to price movements.

Behavioral Biases at Play

Several cognitive biases reinforce the human nature of market cycles:

- **Herd behavior:** Individuals mimic the majority, amplifying trends and creating bubbles or crashes.
- **Confirmation bias:** People seek information that validates their preexisting beliefs, reinforcing irrational exuberance or fear.
- **Recency bias:** Recent gains or losses disproportionately influence decisions, driving short-term overreactions.
- **Overconfidence and illusion of control:** Traders misattribute market outcomes to skill, perpetuating risky behavior.

These biases create feedback loops that often have little to do with economic reality and much more to do with collective psychology.

Historical Evidence of Human-Driven Cycles

Looking across history, virtually every major boom and bust has a common pattern:

- **Tulip Mania (1636–1637):** Prices of tulip bulbs skyrocketed due to social hype, not underlying economic growth.
- **Dot-com Bubble (1997–2000):** Investor enthusiasm for technology stocks far outpaced actual revenue or profitability.
- **2008 Financial Crisis:** Overleveraging, optimism, and herd behavior drove the housing bubble, not fundamental stability.

Across asset classes and eras, emotional cycles repeat, demonstrating that human behavior not purely economic indicators dominates market dynamics.

Implications for Traders and Investors

- **Focus on psychology:** Recognizing crowd emotions can offer predictive insight into market movements.
- **Anticipate extremes:** Booms and busts often overshoot, creating opportunities for contrarian strategies.
- **Maintain discipline:** By acknowledging the human-driven nature of cycles, traders can avoid reactive decisions and stick to process-driven strategies.
- **Learn patterns, not numbers:** While fundamentals inform context, understanding recurring emotional patterns is the key to navigating cycles effectively.

Key Insight

Markets are fundamentally mirrors of human psychology. Booms and busts are rarely dictated by economics alone; they are the inevitable outcome of collective emotion, cognitive bias, and social influence. By studying human behavior, traders and investors gain the most reliable lens through which to anticipate and navigate market cycles.

10.3 Emotional Signatures of Each Phase

Every phase of a market cycle carries a distinct set of emotional responses that drive behavior and influence price action. By identifying these emotional signatures, traders and investors can anticipate likely reactions, position strategically, and avoid being swept away by crowd dynamics. Emotional awareness provides an edge that purely analytical methods cannot replicate.

Hope

- **Dominant Emotions:** Curiosity, cautious optimism, anticipation.
- **Behavioral Traits:** Selective accumulation of positions, careful risk-taking, observation of market trends.
- **Market Impact:** Modest price increases; early participants gain advantage as confidence gradually builds.
- **Trader Insight:** Opportunities exist for those willing to act patiently and strategically before broader participation begins.

Euphoria

- **Dominant Emotions:** Exuberance, overconfidence, greed, and fear of missing out (FOMO).
- **Behavioral Traits:** Aggressive buying, ignoring fundamentals, leveraging positions, and chasing momentum.
- **Market Impact:** Rapid price acceleration, overvaluation, formation of speculative bubbles.
- **Trader Insight:** Extreme caution is warranted; contrarian strategies may yield opportunities for disciplined participants.

Fear

- **Dominant Emotions:** Anxiety, doubt, uncertainty.
- **Behavioral Traits:** Partial exits, hesitation to enter trades, increased attention to short-term losses.
- **Market Impact:** Volatility rises, trend reversals may begin, liquidity fluctuates as participants reassess positions.
- **Trader Insight:** Monitor market structure and volume to distinguish temporary corrections from trend reversals.

Capitulation

- **Dominant Emotions:** Desperation, panic, regret, helplessness.
- **Behavioral Traits:** Mass selling, emotional exits, disregard for valuation, abandoning long-term strategies.
- **Market Impact:** Sharp price declines, market overshoots to the downside, extreme volatility.
- **Trader Insight:** Contrarian participants can capitalize on opportunities as smart money quietly accumulates positions for the next recovery.

Recovery

- **Dominant Emotions:** Relief, cautious optimism, renewed confidence.
- **Behavioral Traits:** Gradual buying, careful re-entry, evaluation of risk vs. opportunity.
- **Market Impact:** Stabilization of prices, reduced volatility, groundwork for a new cycle.
- **Trader Insight:** Patient observation and selective participation can establish favorable positions ahead of broader market enthusiasm.

Key Insight

Every market cycle is a story of collective emotion. By understanding the emotional signatures of Hope, Euphoria, Fear, Capitulation, and Recovery, traders can anticipate likely behaviors, align their strategies with market psychology, and navigate volatility with foresight rather than reaction. Emotional intelligence in markets is as critical as analytical skill.

Chapter 11

The Anatomy of a Bubble

Bubbles are perhaps the most dramatic and emotionally charged phenomena in financial markets. They represent periods when collective optimism, greed, and social dynamics push prices far beyond what fundamentals can justify. From the tulip mania of the 17th century to the recent surges in technology and cryptocurrency markets, bubbles illustrate how human psychology repeatedly drives extreme market behavior.

In this chapter, we explore the anatomy of a bubble through historical and contemporary case studies, highlighting common patterns and psychological triggers. We will examine the pervasive belief in the "this time is different" syndrome, the mechanisms through which greed amplifies market moves, and how early recognition of these emotional echoes can provide strategic opportunities. By studying bubbles as both social and psychological constructs, traders and investors can learn to identify unsustainable extremes, protect capital, and potentially capitalize on moments when the crowd's behavior diverges from rational fundamentals.

11.1 Case Studies: Tulip Mania, Dot-com, Crypto, AI Stocks

Understanding bubbles is easier when viewed through concrete examples. Across history, seemingly unrelated markets have exhibited remarkably similar patterns, driven not by fundamentals, but by collective psychology. Studying these case studies helps traders recognize recurring emotional dynamics and anticipate potential market extremes.

Tulip Mania (1636–1637)

Tulip Mania in the Netherlands is one of the earliest documented market bubbles. Tulip bulbs, especially rare varieties, became highly sought-after luxury items. Prices soared to extraordinary levels, often exceeding the annual income of skilled laborers.

- **Psychology:** Fear of missing out, social proof, and herd behavior drove speculative buying.
- **Behavior:** Traders and investors purchased bulbs not for utility or consumption, but purely for resale at higher prices.
- **Outcome:** When the market sentiment shifted, panic selling ensued, and prices collapsed, leaving many financially ruined.
- **Lesson:** Even assets with no intrinsic financial value can become instruments of mass speculation when collective emotion dominates.

Dot-com Bubble (1997–2000)

During the late 1990s, technology stocks, particularly internet-based companies, experienced exponential price increases despite limited profitability or revenue.

- **Psychology:** Investors were captivated by narratives of a "new economy," convinced that traditional valuation metrics no longer applied.
- **Behavior:** Overconfidence, herd participation, and aggressive speculation fueled rapid market expansion.
- **Outcome:** When companies failed to meet lofty expectations, stock prices plummeted, wiping out trillions in market value.
- **Lesson:** Narratives can override fundamentals, and mass belief in innovation or disruption can create unsustainable price surges.

Cryptocurrency Surges (2017, 2020–2021)

Bitcoin, Ethereum, and other cryptocurrencies have experienced multiple dramatic price run-ups, driven by speculation, media hype, and social enthusiasm.

- **Psychology:** FOMO, greed, and the allure of exponential gains dominated decision-making.
- **Behavior:** Retail investors rushed in without understanding the technology or market dynamics; leveraged positions amplified volatility.
- **Outcome:** Sharp corrections followed periods of mania, often erasing significant gains in weeks.
- **Lesson:** Novel markets attract emotional extremes; social contagion can amplify irrational exuberance.

AI Stocks and Emerging Technologies (2023–Present)

The rise of AI-related equities has produced rapid price appreciation reminiscent of prior bubbles.

- **Psychology:** Investors are captivated by transformational narratives, projecting limitless potential into early-stage companies.
- **Behavior:** Buying accelerates on hype, media coverage, and peer influence, often ignoring fundamentals or risk.
- **Outcome:** While some companies achieve long-term success, others face steep corrections once expectations overshoot reality.
- **Lesson:** Emotional momentum often precedes rational evaluation; understanding the psychological drivers behind adoption and hype is key to navigating new technology markets.

Key Insight

> *Across centuries and asset classes, the anatomy of a bubble remains consistent: collective hope escalates into euphoria, fueled by greed, social proof, and the illusion of inevitability. Recognizing these patterns enables traders to anticipate extremes, manage risk, and identify opportunities where the crowd's emotion diverges from reality.*

11.2 The "This Time is Different" Syndrome

One of the most dangerous psychological traps in financial markets is the belief that "this time is different." During bubbles, participants convince themselves that traditional rules, valuation metrics, or historical patterns no longer apply. This mindset amplifies risk, fuels speculation, and often prolongs the mania until reality intervenes.

Origins of the Syndrome

The "this time is different" belief emerges from a combination of factors:

- **Innovation or new narratives:** Novel technologies or markets create a sense that past lessons are irrelevant. For example, the rise of the internet, blockchain, or AI prompts investors to dismiss historical valuation principles.
- **Recency bias:** Recent gains reinforce the idea that the upward trend will continue indefinitely, even in the face of underlying weaknesses.

- **Social proof and herd behavior:** When everyone around you is succeeding or profiting, it is psychologically easy to assume the trend is justified and safe.
- **Overconfidence and ego:** Investors want to believe they are smarter than predecessors who missed similar opportunities or suffered losses in prior cycles.

Behavioral Consequences

Believing "this time is different" drives a range of behaviors that exacerbate bubbles:

- Ignoring risk management and overleveraging positions.
- Chasing price momentum without evaluating fundamentals.
- Dismissing warnings, skepticism, or contrary evidence as irrelevant or outdated.
- Increasing exposure as fear of missing out grows, which further inflates prices.

Historical Examples

- **Tulip Mania:** Speculators believed rare tulips would always rise in value due to social prestige, ignoring the absence of intrinsic financial utility.
- **Dot-com Bubble:** Investors assumed internet companies could achieve infinite growth, disregarding earnings, profitability, or business fundamentals.
- **Cryptocurrency Mania:** Enthusiasts proclaimed that blockchain assets were immune to traditional valuation concerns, often stating that previous crashes would not repeat.

Recognizing and Countering the Syndrome

Traders and investors can protect themselves by:

- Regularly questioning assumptions: "Am I ignoring fundamentals because of excitement or narrative?"
- Studying historical bubbles to identify recurring patterns and emotional cues.
- Maintaining strict risk management rules, including position sizing and stop-loss strategies.
- Seeking objective feedback from mentors, peers, or market indicators rather than relying solely on personal conviction.

Key Insight

> *The belief that "this time is different" is a psychological amplifier of bubbles. It blinds participants to risk, reinforces greed, and delays rational exits. Recognizing this mindset as a recurring emotional bias allows traders and investors to act deliberately, align decisions with reality, and avoid being swept away by collective delusion.*

11.3 Recognizing the Echo of Greed

Greed is the engine that drives bubbles, market manias, and many extreme price movements. Unlike rational investment motives, greed is emotional, contagious, and often amplified by social and technological forces. Recognizing its echo the subtle and overt signs that collective desire for profit is distorting market behavior is critical for navigating volatility and protecting capital.

The Nature of Greed in Markets

Greed is not merely the desire for wealth; it is the compulsion to pursue gains beyond rational assessment of risk or value. It often manifests as:

- **Overconfidence:** Believing one can time the market perfectly or pick only winners.
- **FOMO (Fear of Missing Out):** Jumping into trades because others are profiting, even when signals are weak.
- **Escalating risk-taking:** Leveraging positions, ignoring stop-losses, or concentrating capital in "hot" assets.
- **Short-term focus:** Prioritizing immediate gains over sustainable, long-term strategies.

Behavioral Indicators of Greed

Traders can detect greed both in themselves and in the broader market through observable behaviors:

- Rapidly rising prices accompanied by heavy media coverage and hype.
- Social reinforcement: forums, social media, and peer discussions emphasizing "get rich quick" narratives.
- Overvaluation: price multiples or asset values that detach from underlying fundamentals.
- Herd accumulation: large numbers of participants entering positions simultaneously, often late in the trend.

Psychological Feedback Loops

Greed tends to create reinforcing feedback loops:

- Rising prices stimulate dopamine release in traders, creating a sense of reward and pleasure.
- Successes, even small or luck-driven, strengthen the illusion of skill and control.
- This leads to more aggressive buying, further inflating the bubble.

Recognizing these loops early allows disciplined traders to take a step back, reassess risk, and avoid being swept up in irrational exuberance.

Case Examples

- **Dot-com Bubble:** Investors ignored lack of profitability, driven by the fear of missing the next big tech stock.
- **Cryptocurrency Mania:** Media-driven hype and social enthusiasm magnified the desire to chase rapid gains.
- **AI Stocks (2023–2024):** Early investors saw exponential potential and FOMO drove massive inflows into overvalued companies.

Strategies to Manage Greed

- Maintain disciplined risk management: position sizing, stop-losses, and portfolio diversification.
- Track emotional triggers: recognize when excitement, envy, or FOMO is influencing decisions.
- Focus on process over outcome: prioritize adherence to strategy rather than chasing quick profits.
- Use reflection tools: journals or checklists to assess whether trades are driven by rational analysis or emotional impulses.

Key Insight

Greed is contagious, persistent, and often subtle. By recognizing its echo through price action, social signals, and internal emotional responses traders can maintain clarity, act rationally, and exploit opportunities where the crowd's desire for profit diverges from underlying value. Awareness of greed is as essential as understanding charts or fundamentals.

Chapter 12

The Anatomy of a Crash

Market crashes are the dramatic flipside of bubbles moments when fear, uncertainty, and collective emotion overwhelm reason, sending prices sharply downward. While booms are fueled by greed and optimism, crashes are powered by panic and loss aversion, often unfolding faster than anyone anticipates. Understanding the anatomy of a crash is crucial for traders and investors seeking to protect capital, recognize turning points, and identify opportunities amidst chaos.

In this chapter, we explore how panic spreads more rapidly than rational analysis, how emotional breakdown interacts with market structure to accelerate declines, and how markets and participants recover after collective trauma. By studying past crashes and the psychological mechanisms that drive them, you will gain insights into the universal patterns of fear, the triggers of mass sell-offs, and strategies to navigate turbulent periods with composure and strategic foresight.

12.1 How Panic Spreads Faster Than Reason

Crashes are not merely a reaction to deteriorating fundamentals they are collective psychological phenomena. Fear propagates through markets like a contagion, often outpacing rational analysis and creating rapid, self-reinforcing declines. Understanding the mechanisms behind this panic is crucial for traders and investors aiming to navigate volatility with awareness and discipline.

The Psychology of Panic

Panic is an acute emotional response triggered by perceived threats or losses. In markets, this perception is often amplified by cognitive biases:

- **Loss aversion:** Humans feel losses more intensely than equivalent gains, prompting quick, emotionally-driven exits.

- **Herd behavior:** Individuals mimic the actions of the majority, believing the crowd knows more than themselves.
- **Recency bias:** Recent price declines heighten anxiety, making participants more likely to sell preemptively.
- **Confirmation bias:** Traders selectively interpret news or indicators to justify exiting positions.

These biases combine to create a feedback loop where selling triggers more selling, accelerating the decline.

Social and Technological Amplifiers

Modern markets are interconnected, and panic spreads faster than ever due to:

- **News media and social platforms:** Sensational headlines, viral posts, and trending discussions amplify fear across global audiences.
- **Algorithmic trading:** Automated systems can exacerbate price moves by executing pre-programmed sell orders in response to market triggers.
- **Peer influence:** Observing friends, colleagues, or social networks exit positions can trigger emotional contagion.

Behavioral Consequences in Market Structure

Panic interacts with market mechanics to produce sharp declines:

- Liquidity dries up as buyers retreat, accelerating downward pressure.
- Bid-ask spreads widen, amplifying volatility and discouraging cautious participants.
- Margin calls and leveraged positions force additional sales, creating cascading effects.

Historical Examples

- **1929 Stock Market Crash:** Herd panic and margin calls accelerated the collapse beyond underlying economic realities.
- **2008 Financial Crisis:** Fear of counterparty default and the collapse of major institutions led to a global cascade of selling.
- **Crypto Corrections (2018, 2022):** Rapid declines were fueled by social contagion, overleveraged positions, and news-driven panic.

Key Insight

> *Panic spreads faster than reason because human emotion reacts instantaneously, while rational analysis lags. Recognizing the psychological and structural drivers of panic allows traders to step back, maintain discipline, and identify opportunities where the crowd's fear overshoots reality. In every crash, understanding the human element is as critical as understanding the charts.*

12.2 Market Structure Meets Emotional Breakdown

A market crash is not solely the product of fear; it is the interaction of human psychology with the structural mechanics of the market. Emotional breakdown among participants amplifies vulnerabilities in market infrastructure, creating conditions where declines accelerate far beyond what fundamentals alone would dictate. Understanding this interplay is essential for navigating crises with composure and strategy.

Liquidity and Panic

Liquidity the availability of buyers and sellers at reasonable prices is the lifeblood of market stability. During emotional breakdowns:

- Buyers retreat, fearing further losses, causing bid prices to fall sharply.
- Sellers overwhelm the limited number of buyers, widening spreads and increasing volatility.
- Illiquid markets exacerbate price swings, turning small negative news into disproportionately large declines.

Leverage and Forced Selling

Leverage magnifies both gains and losses. When emotional panic coincides with leveraged positions:

- Margin calls force participants to sell quickly, adding fuel to declining prices.
- Portfolio deleveraging cascades across multiple market participants, accelerating the downward spiral.
- Emotional stress increases the likelihood of indiscriminate selling rather than strategic exits.

Stop-Loss Cascades

While stop-loss orders are intended to manage risk, during panics they can amplify declines:

- Automated triggers execute simultaneously, creating sudden spikes in sell orders.
- Emotional reactions to initial price drops lead participants to place more stop-losses, compounding the effect.
- Short-term traders may exacerbate volatility, while long-term investors face greater uncertainty about market bottoms.

Information Overload and Emotional Contagion

In modern markets, information flows instantaneously across news, social media, and analytics platforms:

- Rapid dissemination of negative news amplifies fear and triggers emotional selling.
- Rumors or partial information can create disproportionate reactions, often before fundamentals are fully understood.
- The combination of structural triggers (liquidity gaps, stop-losses, leverage) with psychological contagion produces accelerated declines.

Case Example

During the 1987 Black Monday crash:

- Program trading and portfolio insurance strategies triggered mass selloffs.
- Panic amplified by news coverage and the lack of buyers led to a 22% single-day decline in the Dow Jones Industrial Average.
- Structural vulnerabilities combined with emotional breakdown to create one of the most severe market crashes in history.

Key Insight

> *Market structure magnifies the effects of human emotion. Liquidity gaps, leverage, stop-loss cascades, and information flow all interact with panic to create sharp, self-reinforcing declines. Traders who understand how psychology and market mechanics intertwine can anticipate points of extreme stress, manage risk effectively, and even identify opportunities where rational analysis diverges from mass behavior.*

12.3 Rebuilding After Collective Trauma

After a market crash, the immediate danger may subside, but the aftermath often leaves both financial and psychological scars. Collective trauma from significant losses reshapes market behavior, influences investor sentiment, and alters risk perception. Understanding the recovery phase is crucial for participants who aim to navigate post-crash opportunities with clarity and discipline.

Emotional Recovery

Market participants experience a range of emotional responses following a crash:

- **Fear and caution:** Many investors become risk-averse, hesitant to re-enter markets even when opportunities arise.
- **Regret and guilt:** Traders dwell on missed exits or poor decisions, which can cloud judgment in future trades.
- **Distrust:** Confidence in market mechanisms, advisors, or even personal decision-making can erode temporarily.

Recognizing these emotional responses as natural allows for structured reflection and gradual rebuilding of confidence.

Market Recovery Dynamics

Post-crash markets often exhibit characteristic recovery patterns:

- **Volatility persists:** Early recovery phases can see wild swings as liquidity returns gradually and sentiment oscillates between fear and hope.
- **Capitulation lows:** Prices may reach temporary troughs before stabilizing, creating opportunities for disciplined investors.
- **Narrative shifts:** Media and public perception often frame recovery as cautious optimism, which influences trading behavior and capital allocation.

Understanding these dynamics enables participants to distinguish between noise and genuine market signals.

Behavioral Lessons from Crashes

Crashes provide invaluable lessons about human nature in markets:

- **Humility is essential:** Recognizing the limits of control and the inevitability of uncertainty prevents overconfidence in future trades.
- **The importance of preparation:** Pre-established risk management strategies and contingency plans mitigate the emotional and financial impact of crises.
- **Behavioral patterns repeat:** Emotional cycles of fear, panic, and greed recur, offering the opportunity to apply lessons learned from previous crashes.

Strategic Re-entry

Rebuilding in the aftermath of a crash requires a disciplined, psychologically aware approach:

- **Reassess risk tolerance:** Align portfolio exposure with both financial goals and emotional capacity.
- **Start small:** Gradually re-enter positions to rebuild confidence and experience the market without overwhelming exposure.
- **Use reflection and journaling:** Document decisions, emotional responses, and lessons learned to strengthen self-awareness.
- **Identify asymmetric opportunities:** Crashes often create undervalued assets, but careful analysis is essential to separate opportunity from residual risk.

Key Insight

Recovery after a crash is as much about emotional mastery as financial strategy. By understanding the psychological scars left by collective trauma, recognizing recurring behavioral patterns, and re-entering markets with discipline and awareness, traders and investors can transform past losses into lessons, and fear into informed opportunity. The market, like human nature, rebuilds and evolves but only for those who observe, reflect, and act consciously.

Chapter 13

Behavioral Market Archetypes

Markets are not abstract entities they are reflections of collective human behavior. Just as psychologists categorize personality types to understand individual behavior, we can classify traders and investors into archetypes to anticipate their actions, reactions, and emotional tendencies. Recognizing these behavioral patterns is invaluable: it helps you predict market dynamics, manage risk, and refine your own decision-making process.

In this chapter, we explore four primary market archetypes the Gambler, the Prophet, the Fearful Follower, and the Silent Smart Money. Each archetype exhibits distinct psychological tendencies, trade behaviors, and emotional triggers. By understanding the motivations and pitfalls of these archetypes, you can better navigate market cycles, avoid common emotional traps, and even identify opportunities created by others' predictable behavior.

We also provide actionable guidance to identify your own archetype. Self-awareness is the first step toward controlling impulsive reactions and leveraging your strengths while mitigating your weaknesses. By knowing both yourself and the archetypes around you, you gain a strategic edge in the complex, emotion-driven environment of financial markets.

13.1 The Gambler

The Gambler archetype is one of the most recognizable figures in financial markets. Driven by thrill, risk-taking, and the allure of quick rewards, this trader often prioritizes excitement over analysis. While occasional wins may reinforce confidence, the Gambler is highly susceptible to emotional swings, impulsive decisions, and catastrophic losses.

Psychological Traits

The Gambler exhibits several distinct psychological tendencies:

- **High risk tolerance:** Willing to stake significant capital on uncertain outcomes, often ignoring probability and risk-reward analysis.
- **Chasing excitement:** Trading decisions are influenced by adrenaline, novelty, or the "rush" of potentially large gains.
- **Illusion of control:** Believes they can outsmart the market through timing, intuition, or luck, underestimating randomness.
- **Recency bias and overconfidence:** Wins, especially early ones, reinforce the perception of skill, leading to bigger, riskier bets.

Typical Behaviors in Markets

The Gambler often engages in patterns that make them predictable:

- Frequent speculative trades without thorough analysis.
- Overleveraging positions to magnify potential returns.
- Rapid entry and exit cycles, reacting more to emotion than strategy.
- Ignoring fundamental or technical indicators if they conflict with gut feelings.

Market Impact

The collective actions of Gambler-type traders can amplify volatility:

- Excessive speculation contributes to bubbles, as thrill-seekers drive prices beyond rational value.
- Panic selling in downturns accelerates crashes, as impulsive decisions override disciplined risk management.
- Herd behavior among gamblers can distort sentiment and exaggerate market trends.

Managing or Anticipating the Gambler Archetype

For traders and investors, understanding the Gambler archetype offers strategic advantages:

- **Identify signals:** Notice when rapid price moves are fueled by excitement rather than fundamentals.

- **Avoid emotional traps:** Resist the urge to mimic Gambler behavior; stick to risk management rules.
- **Capitalize on patterns:** Informed participants can exploit overextensions created by impulsive trades.
- **Self-reflection:** Determine if you exhibit Gambler tendencies and implement measures position sizing, checklists, and reflection to maintain discipline.

Key Insight

The Gambler thrives on excitement, risk, and short-term wins, but their behavior creates predictable patterns in the market. Recognizing this archetype, in oneself or others, allows disciplined traders to avoid emotional pitfalls, anticipate volatility, and leverage opportunities arising from impulsive decisions.

13.2 The Prophet

The Prophet archetype represents traders or investors who are driven by vision, conviction, and often contrarian thinking. Unlike the Gambler, the Prophet is less motivated by immediate thrills and more by the belief that they have insight into long-term trends, narratives, or transformative market shifts. Their actions can influence sentiment, validate new paradigms, and occasionally create waves that reshape market expectations.

Psychological Traits

Key psychological tendencies of the Prophet include:

- **Visionary thinking:** Sees potential trends, technologies, or market shifts before the broader market recognizes them.
- **High conviction:** Strong belief in their analysis or narrative, often holding positions through volatility and skepticism.
- **Contrarian mindset:** Willing to act against the majority if their research or insight supports it.
- **Emotional resilience:** Can withstand criticism, short-term losses, and social pressure without succumbing to panic.

Typical Behaviors in Markets

The Prophet's approach to markets is distinct:

- Taking positions based on long-term trends or transformative ideas rather than immediate price action.
- Willingness to hold positions through temporary market irrationality or noise.
- Communicating insights to peers, sometimes influencing collective sentiment and creating followership.
- Balancing analytical rigor with intuition, leveraging both data and narrative understanding.

Market Impact

Prophets can shape markets subtly or dramatically:

- Early adoption and conviction can validate emerging assets or technologies, driving adoption and price momentum.
- Contrarian positions can stabilize or destabilize markets depending on timing and market sentiment.
- Their credibility, once established, can create waves of follower behavior that amplify trends or bubbles.

Managing or Learning from the Prophet Archetype

For traders and investors:

- **Observe conviction without blindly following:** Study the rationale behind positions rather than acting solely on reputation.
- **Identify early signals:** Recognize when visionary traders are influencing market narratives and adjust strategy accordingly.
- **Emulate disciplined vision:** Learn from their research methodology, risk awareness, and emotional resilience.
- **Self-assessment:** Determine if you are naturally a Prophet archetype and develop structures to avoid overconfidence or isolation.

Key Insight

> *The Prophet blends vision, conviction, and contrarian insight to anticipate market trends that others overlook. Understanding this archetype helps traders recognize long-term narratives, anticipate behavioral impacts on price action, and develop disciplined strategies that benefit from foresight rather than impulse.*

13.3 The Fearful Follower

The Fearful Follower archetype is defined by hesitation, caution, and a tendency to react to the crowd rather than act proactively. Unlike the Gambler, who seeks risk, or the Prophet, who pursues conviction, the Fearful Follower is highly sensitive to market sentiment, social proof, and the actions of others. Their behavior is primarily reactive, often resulting in late entries, premature exits, and suboptimal trading outcomes.

Psychological Traits

Key psychological tendencies of the Fearful Follower include:

- **High risk aversion:** Reluctant to commit capital without strong reassurance from trends or social validation.
- **Herd dependency:** Looks to the crowd for cues, believing the collective wisdom is superior to individual judgment.
- **Anxiety-driven decision-making:** Fear of loss dominates, leading to indecision or overcautious strategies.
- **Overreliance on confirmation:** Seeks repeated signals or endorsements before taking action.

Typical Behaviors in Markets

The Fearful Follower often exhibits predictable market behaviors:

- Late entry into rising trends, missing early gains.
- Selling too quickly during market downturns, even when fundamentals remain strong.
- Hesitation to take positions without visible confirmation from influential traders or media sentiment.
- Frequent switching between strategies based on perceived crowd behavior.

Market Impact

While individually cautious, the Fearful Follower's collective behavior can have pronounced effects:

- Contributes to market momentum when many join trends simultaneously, amplifying rallies or declines.
- Accelerates panic during downturns, reinforcing emotional contagion and herd selling.

- Often exacerbates volatility by acting late, adding sudden bursts of buying or selling pressure.

Strategies to Navigate or Anticipate Fearful Followers

Understanding the Fearful Follower archetype provides actionable advantages:

- **Anticipate delayed reactions:** Early movers can identify opportunities created by late followers entering or exiting positions.
- **Avoid overreliance on crowd signals:** Maintain independent analysis to prevent reactive mistakes.
- **Leverage for contrarian strategies:** Recognize when excessive caution is driving prices, creating potential value opportunities.
- **Self-reflection:** Identify if you exhibit Fearful Follower tendencies and implement structured decision-making, checklists, and reflection to counteract anxiety-driven behavior.

Key Insight

> *The Fearful Follower reacts to market sentiment rather than shaping it. By recognizing this archetype, traders can anticipate delayed crowd behavior, avoid reactive mistakes, and capitalize on opportunities created by collective hesitation and emotional caution. Awareness of this archetype helps transform fear-driven patterns into strategic insight.*

13.4 The Silent Smart Money

The Silent Smart Money archetype represents the disciplined, strategic, and often understated participants in the market typically institutional investors, hedge funds, or highly informed individuals. Unlike the Gambler or the Fearful Follower, the Silent Smart Money operates quietly, letting their analysis, timing, and execution speak for them. Their influence is profound yet often invisible, shaping trends subtly and consistently over time.

Psychological Traits

Key psychological tendencies of the Silent Smart Money include:

- **Patience and discipline:** Willing to wait for optimal setups rather than chasing short-term moves.
- **Low emotional reactivity:** Decisions are driven by analysis, probability, and risk management rather than fear or greed.

- **Strategic vision:** Focused on long-term objectives and asymmetric opportunities rather than immediate gratification.
- **Observational acuity:** Tracks market sentiment and behavioral patterns of other participants to anticipate moves.

Typical Behaviors in Markets

The Silent Smart Money behaves in ways that are deliberate and calculated:

- Entering or exiting positions quietly to avoid triggering crowd reactions.
- Using size, timing, and tactics to minimize market impact.
- Leveraging behavioral insights to exploit emotional overreactions of other archetypes.
- Maintaining consistent strategies even when the crowd panics or becomes euphoric.

Market Impact

Though often unseen, the Silent Smart Money shapes markets in measurable ways:

- Provides stability by absorbing excess volatility caused by impulsive participants.
- Initiates subtle trend changes that become clear only after the fact.
- Profits from the predictable emotional cycles of other archetypes (Gambler, Prophet, Fearful Follower).
- Acts as a counterbalance to herd-driven extremes, sometimes preventing bubbles or mitigating crashes.

Lessons for Retail Traders

Understanding the Silent Smart Money archetype offers actionable insights:

- **Observe quietly:** Focus on market structure, volume, and flow rather than short-term chatter.
- **Emulate discipline:** Develop patience, risk management, and adherence to strategy.
- **Leverage behavioral understanding:** Identify the emotional cycles of others to position asymmetrically.
- **Avoid noise:** Resist impulsive actions triggered by media hype or social sentiment.

Key Insight

The Silent Smart Money moves deliberately, leveraging insight, patience, and emotional intelligence. By understanding and emulating this archetype, traders gain the ability to navigate markets strategically, exploit predictable patterns in crowd behavior, and achieve consistent results while avoiding the pitfalls of impulsive trading. Awareness of this archetype transforms market observation into a tactical advantage.

13.5 Psychological Profiling of Market Participants

Markets are fundamentally driven by people, and understanding the psychology behind their decisions can provide a crucial edge. Psychological profiling involves categorizing participants based on behavior, emotional tendencies, and decision-making patterns. By recognizing these traits in others and in oneself traders can anticipate actions, interpret price movements, and manage risk more effectively.

Why Profiling Matters

Every trade reflects a human decision, influenced by cognitive biases, emotions, and social dynamics. Profiling participants allows you to:

- Predict likely reactions to news, trends, or market stress.
- Identify emotional extremes such as panic, euphoria, or indecision.
- Spot overreactions or herd behavior that create trading opportunities.
- Align your strategy with broader market psychology instead of isolated price action.

Core Archetypes and Behavioral Patterns

Building on the four primary archetypes Gambler, Prophet, Fearful Follower, and Silent Smart Money profiling involves:

- **The Gambler:** Impulsive, thrill-seeking, risk-loving, prone to exaggerated reactions.
- **The Prophet:** Visionary, confident, contrarian, often guiding sentiment through conviction.
- **The Fearful Follower:** Reactive, anxious, herd-driven, late to trends or early out of positions.

- **The Silent Smart Money:** Disciplined, patient, analytical, leveraging others' emotional cycles strategically.

Each archetype interacts with the market differently, creating observable patterns in volume, price movements, and sentiment waves.

Tools for Profiling Participants

Traders can employ several approaches to understand market psychology:

- **Volume and order flow analysis:** Reveals hidden accumulation or distribution by informed participants.
- **Sentiment indicators:** Surveys, social media, and news tone can gauge crowd mood and extremes.
- **Behavioral checklists:** Track emotional triggers and recurring patterns in yourself and the market.
- **Reflection and journaling:** Document decisions and reactions to identify archetypal behaviors over time.

Applying Profiling in Trading

Effective psychological profiling allows traders to:

- Anticipate market moves before they are obvious from price action alone.
- Identify moments of extreme fear or greed where contrarian opportunities exist.
- Adjust personal strategy according to the archetype one embodies, reducing emotional mistakes.
- Combine profiling with technical and fundamental analysis to create a multidimensional trading edge.

Key Insight

> *Markets are reflections of human behavior, and every price movement carries a psychological signature. By profiling participants understanding their emotional tendencies, biases, and decision patterns traders gain foresight, control, and a strategic advantage. Observing both yourself and others turns human nature into a tangible market edge.*

Actionable Insight: Identify Your Archetype Before Trading

Understanding your own behavioral tendencies is as important as recognizing the patterns of others. Self-awareness allows you to anticipate emotional pitfalls, manage biases, and leverage your strengths. By identifying your archetype, you gain clarity on how you are likely to react under different market conditions, and can design strategies to minimize mistakes and maximize opportunities.

Step 1: Self-Reflection

Start by honestly assessing your natural tendencies:

- Do you seek thrill and risk, or do you prefer cautious, measured moves?
- Are you driven by conviction and vision, or influenced heavily by crowd behavior?
- Do you plan strategically and act patiently, or do you react impulsively to market movements?

Answering these questions will help you place yourself in one of the primary archetypes Gambler, Prophet, Fearful Follower, or Silent Smart Money or a combination thereof.

Step 2: Observe Your Trading Behavior

Keep a detailed trading journal for at least several weeks:

- Note the decisions you make and the emotions driving them.
- Record moments of fear, greed, overconfidence, or hesitation.
- Track patterns: Are you consistently late to trends? Do you chase high-risk setups?

This exercise reveals recurring behavioral patterns that define your archetype.

Step 3: Map Archetype Tendencies to Market Conditions

Understand how your archetype interacts with market cycles:

- **Gambler:** Likely to chase rallies and panic during downturns. Use position sizing and checklists to temper impulsivity.
- **Prophet:** May hold contrarian positions too long or ignore crowd signals. Balance conviction with risk management.

- **Fearful Follower:** Often late to enter or exit positions. Plan predefined entries/exits to avoid hesitation.
- **Silent Smart Money:** Generally disciplined, but may miss opportunities due to extreme caution. Monitor emerging setups actively.

Step 4: Implement Behavioral Safeguards

Once your archetype is identified:

- Create rules that counteract emotional weaknesses.
- Use journaling, reflection, and structured decision-making to reinforce strengths.
- Monitor emotional triggers and note deviations from your archetypal behavior.

Step 5: Continuous Evolution

Archetypes are not static. Your trading behavior evolves with experience, market exposure, and self-awareness. Regularly reassess your tendencies to ensure your strategies remain aligned with your current psychological profile.

Key Insight

> *Knowing your archetype transforms emotional vulnerability into a strategic advantage. By identifying your tendencies, observing patterns, and implementing safeguards, you gain clarity, discipline, and foresight turning self-awareness into one of your most powerful trading edges.*

Part IV

The Trader's Inner Game

Chapter 14

The Self as the Edge

In the world of trading, many focus on strategies, indicators, and market timing, believing that technical mastery alone can produce consistent profits. Yet the truth is more profound: the greatest edge in any market is not external it resides within the trader. Your mindset, self-awareness, and emotional discipline define how effectively you can execute even the most sophisticated strategies.

This chapter explores why **mindset is more important than method**, and how cultivating self-awareness becomes a form of alpha. By understanding your psychological tendencies, managing impulses, and mastering your inner responses to uncertainty, you transform trading from a purely analytical endeavor into an exercise in self-mastery.

We will examine how recognizing your strengths and weaknesses, regulating emotions, and embracing a disciplined mental framework allows you to navigate volatility with clarity and confidence. Trading becomes not just a pursuit of profit, but a pathway to personal growth, resilience, and strategic advantage.

14.1 Mindset above Method

Trading is often portrayed as a mechanical skill: identify the right setup, follow the signals, and execute flawlessly. While strategy and technical knowledge are important, they are secondary to the mental framework that governs decision-making. A brilliant method executed with poor emotional control or cognitive bias can lead to catastrophic losses, whereas a sound mindset can turn even imperfect strategies into profitable outcomes.

The Primacy of Mindset

Mindset is the internal lens through which all market data, signals, and information are interpreted. It determines:

- **Risk perception:** How much capital you allocate, how you size positions, and your tolerance for drawdowns.
- **Decision speed:** Whether you act decisively in opportunities or hesitate out of fear.
- **Emotional regulation:** The ability to remain calm during volatility and avoid impulsive reactions.
- **Learning agility:** How you process mistakes, adapt strategies, and refine your approach over time.

A trader with the right mindset treats losses as data rather than personal failures, and views profits as confirmation, not ego. This mental discipline ensures consistent application of strategy, even under extreme market stress.

Mindset as a Competitive Edge

Markets are populated by participants with varying skill, knowledge, and emotional control. By cultivating a resilient, disciplined mindset, you gain an edge over others who:

- React impulsively to fear or greed.
- Overtrade in pursuit of excitement.
- Misinterpret noise as signal due to emotional bias.
- Succumb to cognitive biases such as overconfidence, confirmation bias, or anchoring.

Your mindset allows you to remain objective, detach from short-term outcomes, and consistently act in alignment with probabilities rather than emotions.

Developing a Mindset-First Approach

To prioritize mindset over method:

- **Self-awareness:** Regularly assess emotional triggers, biases, and habitual responses.
- **Reflection:** Use journaling or mental checklists to monitor decisions and learn from patterns.
- **Patience and discipline:** Wait for high-probability setups; avoid forcing trades to satisfy ego or boredom.
- **Detachment:** Accept that losses are inevitable and focus on long-term consistency rather than short-term perfection.

Key Insight

> *In trading, the greatest edge is not found in charts, indicators, or systems it is found in the mind. A disciplined, resilient, and self-aware mindset transforms strategies into consistent results, turning emotional control and clarity into your most powerful competitive advantage.*

14.2 Self-awareness as Alpha

In financial markets, "alpha" is commonly thought of as the excess return generated over a benchmark. Yet the most sustainable and powerful form of alpha is internal it comes from self-awareness. Understanding your own psychology, emotional triggers, cognitive biases, and behavioral tendencies allows you to make decisions with clarity, avoid predictable mistakes, and act consistently under pressure.

Why Self-awareness Matters

Markets are reflections of collective human behavior, but your personal reactions determine whether you profit or lose. Without self-awareness:

- You may overtrade in response to fear or greed.
- Cognitive biases such as confirmation bias, anchoring, or loss aversion dominate your decisions.
- Emotional swings cause premature exits or impulsive entries.
- You fail to learn from mistakes, repeating errors in cycles.

By contrast, a self-aware trader recognizes these tendencies and can implement structures and mental strategies to mitigate them.

Components of Self-awareness in Trading

Self-awareness as alpha involves three core dimensions:

- **Emotional Insight:** Understanding your reactions to gains, losses, uncertainty, and volatility.
- **Cognitive Clarity:** Recognizing how biases influence perception, judgment, and decision-making.
- **Behavioral Patterns:** Tracking habitual responses in different market conditions to identify recurring strengths and weaknesses.

Developing these components transforms intuition into actionable insight and turns emotional intelligence into a tangible market advantage.

Practical Applications

- **Trading Journals:** Document not only trades but also emotional states, rationale, and reactions to market events.
- **Self-Reflection Exercises:** Regularly review decisions to identify patterns, strengths, and recurring mistakes.
- **Bias Awareness:** Maintain a "bias log" noting when emotions or assumptions skew your judgment.
- **Emotional Regulation Tools:** Meditation, breathing exercises, and cognitive defusion techniques help maintain composure during volatility.

The Edge of Self-awareness

Self-awareness allows you to:

- React with discipline rather than impulse.
- Avoid emotional traps like revenge trading, FOMO, or panic selling.
- Anticipate how your archetype interacts with market cycles.
- Adapt strategies dynamically, turning psychological insight into actionable alpha.

Key Insight

> *True alpha is internal. By cultivating self-awareness, traders convert introspection into insight, emotion into discipline, and recurring behavioral patterns into a sustainable edge. Understanding yourself becomes the foundation for consistently outperforming both markets and your own impulsive tendencies.*

14.3 Trading as Self-Mastery

Trading is not merely a technical exercise of reading charts, analyzing fundamentals, or executing strategies it is a continuous journey of self-mastery. The market acts as a mirror, reflecting your habits, biases, fears, and desires. By treating trading as a discipline for personal growth, you cultivate resilience, emotional control, and strategic clarity that extend far beyond financial outcomes.

The Market as a Mirror

Every trade exposes aspects of your character:

- **Fear and Greed:** Revealed in impulsive entries, overtrading, or premature exits.
- **Patience and Discipline:** Seen in waiting for high-probability setups and adhering to risk management rules.
- **Cognitive Biases:** Anchoring, confirmation bias, and overconfidence manifest through repeated mistakes.

Recognizing these reflections allows you to confront weaknesses and reinforce strengths, transforming trading into a laboratory for self-improvement.

Principles of Self-Mastery in Trading

To approach trading as self-mastery, cultivate the following principles:

- **Discipline:** Execute plans consistently, even when emotions urge deviation.
- **Patience:** Wait for opportunities with asymmetric reward-to-risk potential rather than forcing trades.
- **Emotional Regulation:** Maintain composure under stress, viewing losses as learning and gains as validation, not ego.
- **Reflection:** Regularly analyze decisions, emotional responses, and market outcomes to identify recurring patterns.
- **Continuous Improvement:** Treat each trade as feedback for refining both strategy and self-awareness.

Integration with Strategy

Self-mastery amplifies the effectiveness of any trading method:

- Decisions become less reactive and more rational.
- Emotional resilience reduces the likelihood of catastrophic errors.
- Consistency improves, allowing compounding of both performance and psychological growth.
- Awareness of your psychological tendencies informs position sizing, risk allocation, and trade execution.

The Long-Term Perspective

Trading as self-mastery reframes losses, volatility, and setbacks as opportunities for growth. Over time, the trader who masters themselves:

- Gains clarity in decision-making under uncertainty.
- Develops patience to wait for optimal setups rather than succumbing to impulsivity.
- Builds confidence grounded in process rather than short-term outcomes.
- Achieves consistent results by aligning psychological strengths with strategic execution.

Key Insight

> *Trading is ultimately an exercise in self-mastery. By observing your reactions, regulating impulses, and aligning mindset with strategy, you transform the market from a source of stress and unpredictability into a mirror for personal growth. Master yourself, and you master the market.*

Chapter 15

Discipline & Emotional Regulation

In trading, knowledge alone is never enough. The most carefully crafted strategies and sophisticated analysis are powerless if the trader cannot manage impulses, regulate emotions, and maintain composure under stress. This chapter explores the neuroscience of self-control, practical methods to build emotional resilience, and actionable techniques to prevent emotions from sabotaging decisions.

Discipline is the bridge between strategy and execution it ensures that well-laid plans survive the turbulence of real markets. Emotional regulation is the shield that protects traders from fear, greed, and frustration, allowing decisions to be made rationally rather than reactively. By understanding the mechanisms behind impulse control and practicing tools like meditation, journaling, and cognitive defusion, traders can develop the mental armor necessary to navigate uncertainty with confidence.

This chapter is designed to provide both the science and the practice: understanding why impulses arise, how emotions influence behavior, and which exercises and frameworks can strengthen your psychological resilience. Mastering discipline and emotional regulation transforms trading from a stressful endeavor into a deliberate, controlled, and sustainable pursuit.

15.1 Neuroscience of Impulse Control

Impulse control is the foundation of disciplined trading. Every impulsive trade, emotional reaction, or premature exit reflects the brain's natural wiring, shaped by evolution to prioritize immediate reward and survival. Understanding the neuroscience behind these impulses allows traders to anticipate, recognize, and manage them effectively, transforming emotional vulnerability into a strategic advantage.

The Brain and Decision-Making

The human brain is divided into multiple systems that influence decision-making:

- **Prefrontal Cortex (PFC):** Often called the brain's "executive center," the PFC governs planning, judgment, and inhibition. A strong, well-regulated PFC enables traders to pause, analyze, and execute decisions deliberately rather than reactively.
- **Limbic System:** This older brain structure drives emotion, motivation, and reward processing. The amygdala, a key part of the limbic system, triggers fear and stress responses, often overriding rational thought during volatility.
- **Dopaminergic Pathways:** Dopamine reinforces behavior by rewarding perceived success or excitement. In trading, dopamine surges during profits or thrilling setups, creating a feedback loop that can lead to overtrading or risk-seeking behavior.

Impulse Triggers in Trading

Impulses arise when emotional circuits dominate rational thought. Common triggers include:

- Sudden market volatility or unexpected news.
- Chasing a perceived "missed opportunity" or fear of missing out (FOMO).
- Overconfidence after a winning streak.
- Cognitive biases such as loss aversion, confirmation bias, or anchoring.

Recognizing these triggers is the first step toward controlling reactions before they translate into costly decisions.

Techniques to Strengthen Impulse Control

- **Delayed Execution:** Force a pause before entering or exiting trades minutes or even seconds can prevent reactive decisions.
- **Predefined Rules:** Establish position sizes, entry/exit criteria, and stop-loss levels in advance to reduce reliance on emotional judgment.
- **Mindfulness Training:** Develop awareness of present-moment sensations, thoughts, and urges without acting on them.
- **Stress Reduction:** Adequate sleep, nutrition, exercise, and breathing techniques improve prefrontal cortex function and emotional regulation.

Practical Implications for Traders

By applying neuroscience principles to trading:

- Emotional reactivity decreases, allowing more consistent adherence to strategy.
- Cognitive biases are easier to detect and mitigate.
- Risk-taking aligns more closely with probability and planned exposure, not emotional spikes.
- Long-term decision-making improves, creating sustainable trading performance.

Key Insight

> *Impulse control is not about suppressing emotion it is about aligning emotional and rational systems. By understanding how your brain processes fear, reward, and uncertainty, you can strengthen the neural pathways that support disciplined decision-making, turning emotional regulation into a decisive trading advantage.*

15.2 Building Emotional Armor

In trading, knowledge and strategy are insufficient without psychological resilience. Emotional armor is the mental strength that allows traders to navigate volatility, uncertainty, and losses without being overwhelmed by fear, greed, or frustration. It acts as a buffer, preventing emotions from dictating impulsive decisions and enabling consistent execution of well-planned strategies.

What Emotional Armor Is

Emotional armor is not suppression or denial of feelings it is awareness, preparation, and control. It consists of:

- **Resilience:** The ability to recover quickly from setbacks and losses.
- **Composure:** Maintaining calm and clarity in volatile or high-stress situations.
- **Self-Regulation:** Recognizing emotional triggers and deliberately choosing responses.
- **Confidence:** Trusting your process and strategy rather than reacting to market noise.

Why Traders Need Emotional Armor

Markets are inherently unpredictable. Even the most experienced traders encounter losing streaks, unexpected news, or sudden market swings. Without emotional armor, these events can trigger:

- Panic selling or premature exits.
- Overtrading in pursuit of lost opportunities.
- Impulsive risk-taking driven by fear or greed.
- Chronic stress, burnout, or erosion of confidence over time.

Emotional armor allows traders to maintain consistent performance despite these challenges.

Techniques to Build Emotional Armor

- **Predefined Trading Plans:** Clear entry, exit, and risk management rules reduce reliance on reactive emotions.
- **Mental Rehearsal:** Visualize potential scenarios, including losses, to prepare emotionally for real market conditions.
- **Stress Management:** Regular exercise, proper sleep, and nutrition enhance cognitive and emotional stability.
- **Mindfulness and Meditation:** Increase awareness of thoughts and feelings without judgment, improving control over reactions.
- **Reflection and Journaling:** Record emotional states during trades, analyze triggers, and track improvement over time.
- **Adaptive Coping Mechanisms:** Develop strategies to respond constructively to frustration, setbacks, and market noise.

Integrating Emotional Armor into Trading

Emotional armor is most effective when it becomes part of your trading routine. Before each session:

- Review your trading plan and risk limits.
- Perform a brief mindfulness exercise to center focus.
- Acknowledge potential emotional triggers and commit to observing them without reacting impulsively.

During trading:

- Pause before executing trades that provoke strong emotional responses.
- Use your pre-planned rules as anchors when uncertainty arises.
- Reflect after each session to reinforce lessons and strengthen resilience.

Key Insight

Emotional armor does not eliminate risk or uncertainty it equips you to handle them. By building resilience, composure, and self-regulation, traders transform emotional vulnerability into strength, enabling disciplined, consistent, and confident decision-making even under pressure.

15.3 Meditation, Journaling, and Cognitive Defusion Techniques

Mastering emotional regulation in trading requires more than awareness it demands consistent practice. Techniques such as meditation, journaling, and cognitive defusion provide practical tools to observe, manage, and detach from emotional and cognitive reactions, creating clarity and control in high-pressure market environments.

Meditation: Training the Mind

Meditation is a scientifically supported method for enhancing focus, reducing stress, and improving emotional regulation. For traders, meditation:

- Strengthens attention and concentration, allowing better recognition of setups and signals.
- Reduces impulsive reactions to market volatility by calming the limbic system and enhancing prefrontal cortex control.
- Encourages present-moment awareness, preventing rumination on past losses or anxiety about future outcomes.

Practical Exercise: Spend 10–20 minutes daily in focused breathing or guided meditation, observing thoughts and emotions without judgment. Over time, this practice improves composure during volatile trading sessions.

Journaling: Externalizing and Analyzing Thoughts

A trading journal is a tool for reflection and self-awareness. Beyond recording trades, it helps monitor emotional and cognitive patterns:

- Document your rationale for entering and exiting trades.

- Record emotional states before, during, and after trades.
- Note recurring triggers for fear, greed, or overconfidence.
- Review past entries to identify patterns, biases, and opportunities for improvement.

Journaling transforms subjective experiences into actionable data, reinforcing self-awareness and facilitating adaptive learning.

Cognitive Defusion: Detaching from Unhelpful Thoughts

Cognitive defusion, a concept from Acceptance and Commitment Therapy (ACT), teaches traders to separate themselves from intrusive or unhelpful thoughts. Instead of reacting to every anxious or impulsive thought, you observe it as transient and external.

- **Example Technique:** Label thoughts as "just thoughts" (e.g., "I notice the fear of missing out") rather than directives to act.
- Helps prevent emotional hijacking and impulsive decision-making.
- Reinforces awareness that thoughts are not necessarily reality or commands.

Integrating Practices into Trading Routine

A practical routine might include:

- Morning meditation to center focus before market open.
- Keeping a trade journal updated during or immediately after sessions.
- Applying cognitive defusion in real-time: noticing impulses, labeling thoughts, and observing without reacting.
- End-of-day reflection: reviewing emotional states, trading decisions, and lessons learned.

Key Insight

> *Meditation, journaling, and cognitive defusion are not optional extras they are core tools for emotional mastery. By training attention, externalizing patterns, and detaching from reactive thoughts, traders create mental clarity, resilience, and the disciplined mindset necessary to navigate markets consistently and profitably.*

Chapter 16

Patience & Probabilistic Thinking

In financial markets, impatience is one of the most costly enemies of a trader. The desire to act quickly, to chase opportunities, or to force trades often leads to suboptimal decisions and emotional burnout. Yet, the most successful traders understand that waiting is not inaction it is a strategic choice. Patience allows the mind to observe, analyze, and act only when conditions align with probability and risk-reward logic.

Coupled with patience is the mindset of probabilistic thinking. Markets are inherently uncertain, and no outcome is guaranteed. Thinking in probabilities rather than absolutes enables traders to make decisions based on expected value, assess risk rationally, and remain composed when outcomes deviate from expectations. It transforms the market from a source of anxiety into a system of calculated opportunities.

This chapter explores how to cultivate patience, recognize asymmetric setups with favorable risk-reward profiles, and embrace uncertainty as a liberating force. By learning to wait, think in odds, and accept that unpredictability is a constant, traders can align their actions with probability, reduce emotional reactivity, and gain a sustainable edge in the markets.

16.1 Waiting for Asymmetric Setups

In trading, not all opportunities are created equal. An asymmetric setup occurs when the potential reward significantly outweighs the potential risk. Recognizing and waiting for these setups is the hallmark of disciplined and successful trading, allowing traders to maximize expected value while minimizing exposure to unnecessary risk.

Understanding Asymmetry

Asymmetry is the imbalance between upside potential and downside risk. For example:

- A trade where you risk 1*topotentiallygain*5 is highly asymmetric.
- A trade with a 1:1 risk-reward ratio may offer limited opportunity and higher stress for the same exposure.

Focusing only on opportunities with favorable asymmetry allows traders to capitalize on high-probability setups while preserving capital during uncertain conditions.

The Importance of Patience

Patience is critical because asymmetric setups do not appear on every chart or every day. Attempting to force trades in the absence of clear asymmetry leads to:

- Overtrading and increased transaction costs.
- Emotional stress from low-probability trades.
- Erosion of capital and confidence over time.

By waiting for setups that clearly meet predefined criteria, traders maintain discipline and optimize long-term performance.

Identifying Asymmetric Setups

Key principles for recognizing asymmetric trades include:

- **High Probability Entry:** Enter trades only when technical, fundamental, or sentiment indicators converge.
- **Favorable Risk-Reward Ratio:** Ensure potential gains exceed potential losses significantly.
- **Clear Exit Strategy:** Know in advance where to take profit and cut losses to protect capital.
- **Market Context:** Consider trend strength, volatility, and macro factors to avoid low-conviction trades.

Psychology of Waiting

Waiting for the right setup requires mental discipline:

- Accepting boredom and discomfort as part of the process.
- Resisting the urge to trade based on emotion or perceived opportunity.
- Viewing inactivity as a strategic decision rather than lost opportunity.

Traders who embrace waiting develop composure, strengthen decision-making, and avoid costly mistakes driven by impatience.

Key Insight

> *Successful trading is less about constant action and more about selective, high-probability engagement. By patiently waiting for asymmetric setups, traders maximize expected value, reduce emotional reactivity, and turn discipline into a sustainable edge.*

16.2 Thinking in Odds, Not Absolutes

One of the most powerful shifts a trader can make is moving from deterministic thinking believing outcomes are certain to probabilistic thinking, where every trade is evaluated in terms of likelihoods and expected value. Markets are inherently uncertain, and no strategy guarantees success on every trade. Thinking in odds allows traders to focus on long-term results rather than the emotional impact of individual wins or losses.

The Principle of Probabilistic Thinking

Probabilistic thinking is about assessing the likelihood of different outcomes and making decisions based on expected value rather than certainty. Key principles include:

- **Expected Value (EV):** Calculate the potential gain or loss of a trade multiplied by its probability. Over many trades, focusing on positive EV setups increases long-term profitability.
- **Risk-Reward Ratios:** Evaluate whether potential rewards justify the risk, even if the trade has only a moderate chance of success.
- **Probability over Certainty:** Accept that losses are inevitable, but profitable strategies produce net gains over time when applied consistently.

Common Pitfalls of Absolute Thinking

Traders who think in absolutes often make mistakes such as:

- Treating a single trade as a "make-or-break" event.
- Overreacting to short-term losses or gains, allowing emotions to drive decisions.
- Chasing certainty where none exists, increasing risk and stress.

By shifting to a probabilistic mindset, traders detach from the illusion of control and make more rational, measured decisions.

Applying Odds in Trading

Practical applications of probabilistic thinking include:

- **Scenario Analysis:** Consider best-case, worst-case, and most-likely outcomes for each trade.
- **Position Sizing:** Adjust exposure according to the probability of success and potential impact on your portfolio.
- **Portfolio Thinking:** Focus on the cumulative performance of many trades rather than obsessing over single outcomes.
- **Decision Frameworks:** Use checklists and criteria that emphasize odds, risk, and reward before acting.

The Psychological Edge

Thinking in odds reduces emotional volatility. By acknowledging uncertainty:

- Fear of losses diminishes because losses are expected and factored into probabilities.
- Greed is tempered by understanding that not every opportunity is worth pursuing.
- Patience and discipline are reinforced, as traders wait for setups that offer favorable probabilities.

Key Insight

Markets are games of probabilities, not certainties. By thinking in odds rather than absolutes, traders make decisions based on expected value, manage risk intelligently, and maintain composure in the face of uncertainty. This mindset transforms volatility from a source of fear into a measurable, manageable, and profitable element of trading.

16.3 Embracing Uncertainty as Liberation

Uncertainty is the essence of financial markets. Prices fluctuate, trends reverse, and unexpected events disrupt even the most carefully planned strategies. While many traders view uncertainty as a threat, the most successful see it as a source of opportunity and freedom. Embracing uncertainty transforms fear into clarity, rigidity into adaptability, and market chaos into strategic advantage.

The Nature of Uncertainty

Markets are complex adaptive systems influenced by countless variables economic data, geopolitical events, investor psychology, and random chance. No trader, no matter how skilled, can predict every move. Accepting this fundamental uncertainty is the first step toward mental liberation:

- Recognize that losses are inevitable and are part of the probabilistic nature of trading.
- Understand that surprise events will always occur; flexibility is key to navigating them.
- Let go of the illusion of absolute control focus instead on controlling your process, not outcomes.

Psychological Benefits of Acceptance

Embracing uncertainty provides profound psychological benefits:

- **Reduces Fear:** When traders accept that outcomes are probabilistic, the fear of unexpected events diminishes. Losses become a natural, manageable component of the trading process.
- **Mitigates Overconfidence:** Accepting unpredictability tempers ego and overestimation of one's control, reducing impulsive or reckless trades.
- **Enhances Flexibility:** Traders remain open to adjusting strategies as conditions change, improving responsiveness and adaptability.

Strategies to Harness Uncertainty

To transform uncertainty into an advantage, traders can apply the following strategies:

- **Focus on Process Over Outcome:** Define clear rules for entry, exit, and risk management. Success is measured by adherence to the process, not individual trade results.

- **Build Robust Risk Management:** Use position sizing, stop-losses, and diversification to protect against unpredictable events.
- **Think in Probabilities:** Evaluate trades based on expected value rather than certainty. Recognize that even high-probability setups can fail.
- **Maintain Emotional Awareness:** Monitor reactions to uncertainty, and use mindfulness, journaling, or cognitive defusion to prevent fear from dictating actions.
- **Seek Opportunities in Chaos:** Volatility and surprise events create mispricings and asymmetric setups embracing uncertainty allows traders to act decisively when others hesitate.

Reframing Uncertainty as Liberation

Rather than seeing uncertainty as a limitation, it can be reframed as freedom:

- You are not bound by expectation you can respond creatively to whatever occurs.
- Each surprise offers information; every volatility spike provides potential opportunity.
- By letting go of attachment to specific outcomes, traders can operate with clarity, composure, and strategic focus.

Key Insight

> *Uncertainty is not an enemy it is a natural condition of markets. By embracing unpredictability, traders liberate themselves from fear, rigid thinking, and emotional bias, transforming the unknown into a source of strategic advantage. The most successful traders do not resist uncertainty; they thrive within it.*

Chapter 17

Cognitive Biases in Trading

Even the most disciplined and well-prepared traders are vulnerable to cognitive biases systematic patterns of thinking that distort judgment and decision-making. These mental shortcuts, while often useful in everyday life, can become costly in financial markets, leading to misjudged risk, overconfidence, and suboptimal trades.

This chapter explores the most common biases that affect traders, including anchoring, recency, hindsight, and confirmation bias. By understanding how these biases influence perception and behavior, traders can develop strategies to recognize, counteract, and even leverage them to their advantage. We will also examine practical tools and techniques that professional traders use to "de-bias" their decision-making process, transforming awareness into consistent, rational action.

Through a combination of psychological insight, real-world examples, and actionable frameworks, this chapter equips readers to navigate the hidden mental forces shaping market behavior and to make clearer, more objective trading decisions.

17.1 Anchoring, Recency, Hindsight, Confirmation Biases

Cognitive biases are systematic errors in thinking that influence judgment and decision-making. In trading, these biases can distort perception, mislead analysis, and trigger emotional reactions that lead to suboptimal outcomes. Understanding the most common biases and their manifestations in financial markets is essential for developing a disciplined, rational approach.

Anchoring Bias

Anchoring occurs when traders rely too heavily on an initial reference point such as a past price, target, or forecast when making decisions.

- **Example:** A stock previously trading at $150 may cause a trader to perceive $140 as "cheap," even if market conditions have fundamentally changed.
- Anchoring can prevent adaptation to new information, leading to holding losing positions or ignoring better opportunities.
- **Market Implication:** Anchored traders may fail to adjust stop-loss levels or misprice risk, resulting in avoidable losses.

Recency Bias

Recency bias is the tendency to give undue weight to the most recent events while discounting historical context or long-term trends.

- **Example:** After a stock rallies for three days, traders might expect the trend to continue indefinitely, ignoring longer-term volatility or mean-reversion patterns.
- This bias leads to chasing momentum, overtrading, or assuming that the recent past will reliably predict the immediate future.
- **Market Implication:** Recency bias can inflate risk exposure and generate emotional trading cycles driven by short-term performance rather than strategy.

Hindsight Bias

Hindsight bias is the tendency to perceive past events as having been predictable after they have occurred.

- **Example:** After a market crash, a trader might claim they "knew it was coming," even though prior analysis was uncertain.
- This creates overconfidence, reduces the perceived need for caution, and can distort learning from past trades.
- **Market Implication:** Hindsight bias fosters overestimation of predictive ability, leading to larger, riskier positions or repeated mistakes.

Confirmation Bias

Confirmation bias occurs when traders seek or interpret information in ways that confirm pre-existing beliefs, while ignoring contradictory evidence.

- **Example:** A trader bullish on a stock may only read positive news, ignoring warning signs such as declining fundamentals or sector weakness.
- This bias reinforces false narratives and can prolong holding losing trades or entering low-probability setups.
- **Market Implication:** Confirmation bias reduces objectivity, diminishes critical thinking, and increases vulnerability to losses.

Recognizing Bias Patterns

By tracking decisions, reviewing trade journals, and reflecting on emotional triggers, traders can identify recurring bias patterns. Awareness is the first step toward mitigation:

- Document decisions and rationale, noting emotional or cognitive influences.
- Compare outcomes against pre-trade analysis to detect distortions caused by bias.
- Develop checklists and rules to counteract natural tendencies, ensuring that each trade aligns with objective criteria rather than subjective perception.

Key Insight

Anchoring, recency, hindsight, and confirmation biases subtly shape every trading decision. By recognizing these cognitive distortions, traders can step back, evaluate information objectively, and implement structured processes that reduce error, improve discipline, and enhance long-term profitability.

17.2 Tools to Neutralize Biases

Understanding cognitive biases is only the first step; the real skill lies in actively countering them. Traders who systematically neutralize biases gain clarity, reduce emotional errors, and make decisions aligned with probability and strategy rather than instinct. This section outlines practical tools and frameworks to minimize the influence of common cognitive distortions.

Trade Journals

Keeping a detailed trade journal is one of the most effective tools for debiasing:

- Record the rationale for every trade, including entry and exit points, risk-reward calculations, and anticipated outcomes.
- Note emotional states and any gut feelings influencing decisions.
- Review past trades regularly to identify patterns of bias, such as overconfidence, anchoring, or recency effects.

Journaling transforms subjective experience into objective data, allowing traders to spot recurring errors and adjust their approach.

Checklists and Decision Frameworks

Structured decision-making helps remove subjectivity:

- Develop pre-trade checklists to ensure all criteria are met before entering a position.
- Include steps to verify risk-reward ratios, confirm alignment with trend, and account for macro conditions.
- Use post-trade checklists to evaluate adherence to rules and identify deviations caused by biases.

Checklists enforce discipline, reduce impulsivity, and standardize decision-making under pressure.

Statistical and Probabilistic Tools

Applying quantitative frameworks counters emotional and cognitive distortions:

- Use historical data to validate patterns instead of relying on anecdotal evidence.
- Apply probabilistic models to assess expected value, risk exposure, and potential outcomes.
- Measure deviations objectively to avoid subjective interpretation or confirmation bias.

Numbers do not eliminate risk, but they provide a neutral lens through which to evaluate trades.

Mindfulness and Reflection Practices

Mental training strengthens awareness of cognitive tendencies:

- Daily mindfulness or meditation enhances the ability to recognize impulsive thoughts.
- Reflective exercises, such as end-of-day reviews, help identify moments when biases influenced decisions.
- Cognitive defusion techniques allow traders to separate thoughts from actions, reducing the power of emotional reactions.

Peer Review and Mentorship

Collaborating with trusted peers or mentors can highlight blind spots:

- Discuss trade rationale with others to detect bias or overconfidence.
- Seek feedback from experienced traders who can provide objective perspectives.
- Engage in scenario analysis and "what-if" exercises to challenge assumptions.

External perspectives serve as reality checks, helping prevent individual biases from going unchecked.

Key Insight

> *Cognitive biases are inevitable, but their impact can be mitigated through disciplined systems. Trade journals, checklists, probabilistic analysis, mindfulness, and peer feedback collectively create a framework that transforms awareness into actionable control, enabling traders to make decisions driven by logic, process, and probability rather than instinct or emotion.*

17.3 How Pros De-bias Their Process

Professional traders and institutional investors understand that cognitive biases are unavoidable. The key to consistent performance lies not in eliminating biases entirely, but in building systems and habits that minimize their influence. This section explores how experienced market participants structure their processes to maintain objectivity, discipline, and clarity under pressure.

Structured Decision-Making

Pros rarely rely solely on intuition. They design robust decision frameworks:

- **Predefined Criteria:** Entry and exit rules, risk-reward thresholds, and stop-loss levels are established before trades are taken.
- **Scenario Planning:** Potential outcomes are mapped in advance, including best-case, worst-case, and most-likely scenarios.
- **Checklists:** Systematic evaluation ensures every trade aligns with objective criteria, reducing impulsive or emotionally driven decisions.

Structured frameworks convert subjective judgment into repeatable, measurable processes.

Continuous Monitoring and Reflection

Pros actively monitor both market behavior and their own psychology:

- **Trade Journals:** Detailed logging of every trade, rationale, and emotional state helps identify recurring cognitive patterns.
- **Bias Audits:** Regular reviews of past decisions highlight tendencies like overconfidence, anchoring, or confirmation bias.
- **Post-Mortem Analysis:** Evaluating wins and losses objectively allows traders to learn without ego interference.

Reflection is an essential feedback loop for continuous improvement.

Quantitative Validation

Experienced traders rely on data-driven methods to reduce subjective errors:

- Historical price data, backtesting, and probabilistic models verify assumptions and signal reliability.
- Risk metrics and volatility analysis provide objective measures, helping to counter emotional overreactions.
- Statistical tracking ensures trades are evaluated based on long-term outcomes rather than isolated successes or failures.

Numbers act as a neutral arbiter, grounding decisions in evidence rather than perception.

Mindset and Emotional Control

De-biasing also requires psychological preparation:

- **Mindfulness Practices:** Meditation and breathing techniques help maintain calm under pressure.
- **Cognitive Defusion:** Separating thoughts from actions prevents impulsive trades driven by fear or greed.
- **Patience:** Professionals wait for high-probability setups rather than reacting to every market movement.

Emotional regulation complements procedural safeguards, creating a holistic defense against cognitive distortion.

Collaborative Checks

Institutional traders often incorporate social systems to mitigate individual bias:

- **Peer Reviews:** Trading decisions are occasionally reviewed by colleagues to identify blind spots.
- **Mentorship:** Guidance from experienced traders reinforces objectivity and provides alternative perspectives.
- **Discussion and Debate:** Constructive critique challenges assumptions and mitigates groupthink.

External feedback provides a safety net, ensuring personal biases do not dominate decision-making.

Key Insight

> *Professional traders accept that cognitive biases cannot be eradicated, but their impact can be systematically reduced. By combining structured decision frameworks, continuous reflection, quantitative validation, emotional discipline, and collaborative checks, pros create an environment where objective reasoning dominates instinct. Mastering these practices transforms awareness into consistent, rational trading performance.*

Chapter 18

The Psychology of Risk

Risk is an inseparable part of trading and investing, yet it is far more psychological than mathematical. Every decision to enter or exit a trade involves assessing uncertainty, managing potential loss, and confronting the emotional impact of outcomes. Understanding the psychology of risk is therefore critical: two traders with identical positions and capital can respond very differently depending on their tolerance for uncertainty, emotional resilience, and perception of potential consequences.

This chapter explores how human cognition and emotion shape risk-taking behavior. We will examine the role of uncertainty tolerance why some traders thrive under volatility while others crumble the importance of position sizing in aligning risk with personal capacity, and why risk is ultimately a perception rather than a fixed numerical quantity. By the end of this chapter, you will gain tools to identify your own risk profile, manage emotional exposure, and make more rational, calculated decisions in the face of uncertainty.

Through practical frameworks, actionable insights, and reflective exercises such as maintaining a "bias journal," this chapter equips traders to observe when emotions skew judgment and transform that awareness into disciplined risk management.

18.1 Understanding Uncertainty Tolerance

Every trader has a unique threshold for uncertainty the level of unpredictability they can endure without making impulsive or emotionally driven decisions. This tolerance profoundly shapes trading behavior, influencing position sizing, risk management, and response to market volatility. Understanding your own uncertainty tolerance is a critical first step toward disciplined and profitable trading.

The Nature of Uncertainty Tolerance

Uncertainty tolerance is not static; it reflects a combination of personality, experience, and cognitive wiring:

- **Personality Traits:** Risk-averse individuals prefer stable, predictable outcomes, while risk-tolerant traders are comfortable with volatility and ambiguity.
- **Experience:** Seasoned traders often develop higher tolerance through repeated exposure to market fluctuations, learning to manage emotional reactions.
- **Evolutionary Wiring:** Human brains are wired to avoid losses and seek safety, a mechanism that can conflict with the calculated risk-taking required in markets.

Recognizing your natural tolerance helps you avoid overextending or underutilizing your trading potential.

Behavioral Manifestations

Uncertainty tolerance influences decision-making in predictable ways:

- **Overreaction to Volatility:** Traders with low tolerance may panic sell during minor drawdowns or abandon high-probability setups.
- **Excessive Risk-Taking:** Those with overly high tolerance may ignore position sizing rules, exposing themselves to catastrophic losses.
- **Decision Paralysis:** Moderate tolerance can still result in hesitation, missed opportunities, or delayed entries and exits due to fear of uncertainty.

By observing these behaviors, traders can calibrate strategies to match psychological comfort and maintain consistent decision-making.

Practical Assessment

To gauge your uncertainty tolerance:

- Simulate trades under varying conditions to observe emotional and cognitive responses.
- Maintain a journal documenting reactions to market swings and unexpected outcomes.
- Adjust position sizes incrementally to align exposure with comfort levels while remaining within objective risk parameters.

Key Insight

> *Understanding your uncertainty tolerance transforms trading from a reactionary process into a deliberate practice. By aligning your risk-taking with your psychological comfort, you maintain composure under volatility, avoid impulsive decisions, and create the foundation for consistent, rational performance.*

18.2 Position Sizing and Emotional Risk Capacity

Position sizing is the bridge between theoretical risk management and practical, psychologically sustainable trading. It determines how much capital to allocate to each trade, balancing potential gains against the trader's tolerance for stress and emotional exposure. Ignoring emotional risk can turn a mathematically sound trade into a disastrous decision if fear, greed, or stress leads to impulsive reactions.

The Concept of Emotional Risk Capacity

Emotional risk capacity refers to the amount of uncertainty or potential loss a trader can endure without deviating from their strategy:

- Traders with low emotional risk capacity may panic during minor drawdowns, leading to premature exits.
- Traders with high capacity may tolerate volatility but risk overconfidence and overexposure if position sizing is misaligned.
- Emotional capacity is dynamic it changes with experience, market conditions, and personal circumstances.

Understanding your emotional limits is as important as calculating capital-based risk.

Position Sizing Techniques

Effective position sizing integrates both objective capital risk and subjective emotional risk:

- **Fixed Fractional Method:** Risk a constant percentage of total capital per trade (e.g., 1–2%). This limits losses and maintains emotional equilibrium.
- **Volatility-Based Sizing:** Adjust position size according to market volatility, reducing exposure in highly unpredictable conditions.

- **Probabilistic Sizing:** Factor in the probability of success, expected value, and potential drawdowns to align risk with expected outcomes.

These methods ensure that trades remain within tolerable limits, preventing emotion-driven deviations.

Aligning Capital and Psychology

Position sizing should reflect both numerical calculations and emotional resilience:

- **Stress Testing:** Simulate scenarios of consecutive losses to determine how much risk your mind can tolerate without panic or rash decisions.
- **Incremental Adjustments:** Gradually increase or decrease exposure based on experience and comfort, avoiding abrupt changes that trigger stress.
- **Self-Awareness Practices:** Monitor heart rate, tension, or emotional reactions during trades to gauge whether position size exceeds psychological capacity.

Traders who respect both capital and emotional limits maintain discipline and consistency.

The Feedback Loop

Position sizing is not static it should evolve as your experience, capital, and psychological tolerance change:

- Review trading outcomes to determine if current sizing induces excessive stress.
- Adjust trade sizes or risk percentages to maintain alignment with your comfort and performance goals.
- Combine with journaling to track emotional responses and refine sizing strategies over time.

Key Insight

Position sizing is not just a mathematical exercise it is a psychological safeguard. By aligning trade size with both capital and emotional capacity, traders protect themselves from panic, impulsivity, and overexposure, creating the conditions for disciplined, consistent, and profitable trading.

18.3 Why Risk is Perception, Not Math

In financial markets, risk is often portrayed as a numerical calculation a percentage chance of loss, standard deviation, or volatility metric. While these measures provide valuable information, they only tell part of the story. The true experience of risk is inherently psychological. Two traders can face the same statistical probability of loss, yet one may act calmly while the other panics. Understanding this distinction between objective risk and perceived risk is crucial for mastering trading psychology.

The Nature of Perceived Risk

Perceived risk arises from the mind's interpretation of uncertainty, loss, and potential outcomes:

- **Subjectivity of Loss:** A 2% loss may feel catastrophic to a trader who lacks confidence or experience, while another may treat it as a minor setback.
- **Emotional Amplification:** Fear, greed, and stress amplify the perception of risk, causing overreactions or overly cautious behavior.
- **Cognitive Filters:** Anchoring, recency, and confirmation biases distort how probabilities and past events are interpreted, altering perceived risk independently of statistical reality.

Perception, therefore, dictates behavior more than the actual numbers on a screen.

Risk vs. Uncertainty

It is important to distinguish between risk (quantifiable probabilities) and uncertainty (unknown or unpredictable factors):

- **Risk:** Can be measured using tools like volatility, stop-loss levels, and probability models.
- **Uncertainty:** Involves unknowns that cannot be precisely quantified, such as unexpected news, market sentiment shifts, or global events.
- Traders' perception of uncertainty often drives decisions more than calculated risk, highlighting the psychological component of trading.

Implications for Decision-Making

When risk is perceived differently by different traders, market behavior becomes as much a reflection of collective psychology as it is of fundamentals:

- Overestimation of risk can lead to missed opportunities, undertrading, or excessive hedging.
- Underestimation of risk can result in overexposure, reckless trades, and large drawdowns.
- Successful traders calibrate their perception, aligning it with objective probabilities while accounting for emotional reactions.

Strategies to Align Perception with Reality

Traders can reduce the gap between perceived and actual risk through structured techniques:

- **Visualization and Scenario Planning:** Mentally rehearsing adverse outcomes prepares the mind to accept losses objectively.
- **Probabilistic Thinking:** Focusing on expected value and probabilities reduces emotional overreactions to individual outcomes.
- **Bias Journals:** Tracking instances where emotions exaggerated or minimized perceived risk helps recalibrate judgment over time.

Key Insight

Risk is not solely a number it is the mind's interpretation of uncertainty and potential loss. Mastery in trading arises from aligning perception with reality, managing emotional amplification, and making decisions grounded in probabilities rather than feelings. When perception is calibrated, fear and greed lose their control over your actions, allowing rational, disciplined trading to prevail.

Actionable Insight: Maintain a Bias Journal

One of the most powerful tools for mastering risk perception and improving trading performance is a bias journal. While many traders track profits and losses, few systematically observe the psychological forces that drive their decisions. A bias journal allows you to record, analyze, and correct emotional and cognitive patterns that skew judgment.

Purpose of a Bias Journal

The bias journal serves several critical functions:

- **Self-Awareness:** By documenting thoughts, feelings, and decisions, you gain clarity on how emotions influence trades.

- **Pattern Recognition:** Over time, recurring cognitive biases such as overconfidence, loss aversion, or FOMO become apparent.
- **Corrective Action:** Identifying biases allows you to implement strategies that neutralize their impact on future decisions.

What to Record

A comprehensive bias journal should capture both quantitative and qualitative information:

- **Trade Details:** Entry and exit points, position size, stop-loss, and take-profit levels.
- **Rationale:** Why you entered the trade, what analysis or indicators influenced your decision.
- **Emotional State:** Record fear, greed, excitement, or doubt experienced before, during, and after the trade.
- **Outcome Reflection:** Evaluate whether emotions influenced deviations from your plan and how the trade outcome aligned with expectations.
- **Bias Identification:** Note any cognitive distortions observed, such as confirmation bias, recency effect, or anchoring.

How to Use the Journal Effectively

- Review entries weekly to detect patterns and recurring emotional triggers.
- Compare trades where emotions were well-managed against trades where biases dominated decisions.
- Implement incremental changes adjust position size, introduce checklists, or employ probabilistic frameworks based on insights from the journal.
- Reflect on long-term trends in behavior to improve risk perception, patience, and consistency.

Psychological Benefits

Maintaining a bias journal strengthens emotional intelligence and self-discipline:

- Enhances mindfulness and moment-to-moment awareness during trades.
- Reduces impulsive reactions by converting emotional experiences into objective data.

- Builds confidence, as decisions become more process-driven rather than emotion-driven.

Key Insight

A bias journal transforms subjective experiences into actionable intelligence. By systematically tracking thoughts, emotions, and cognitive distortions, traders gain unprecedented insight into their own psychology. Over time, this practice not only sharpens decision-making and risk perception but also fosters self-mastery a true edge in the markets.

Part V

Beyond The Chart: Human Nature In Wealth, Power Society

Chapter 19

Money as a Mirror of Morality

Introduction

Money is often misunderstood as a mere tool a neutral medium of exchange, a number on a screen, a symbol of success. But in reality, money functions as a **mirror** reflecting back the deepest layers of our morality, intentions, and self-concept. It doesn't change who we are; it **amplifies** who we already are. The patient become wealthier through discipline. The greedy become poorer through excess. The humble use wealth to create, while the arrogant use it to dominate. In essence, *money is not moral or immoral it's a multiplier of character.*

In trading and investing, this principle is starkly visible. Two traders can hold the same stock, with identical charts and signals, but one trades out of fear while the other trades from clarity. The outcomes, and the legacies, differ not because of the market but because of the **moral and emotional frameworks** driving each decision. Profit-seeking, when detached from ethics, often leads to ruin masked as success. The pursuit of money without moral clarity becomes a race with no finish line where winning feels empty, and losing feels existential.

The **moral dimension of profit** is rarely discussed in financial education. Yet every trade carries a value judgment: *What am I willing to risk, and for what kind of reward?* Ethical asymmetry the imbalance between decision, integrity, and time defines one's ultimate **legacy**. A trader who compromises integrity for short-term gain may profit temporarily, but over time, the compounding effect of moral erosion becomes more destructive than any drawdown.

This chapter explores how wealth and morality intertwine not philosophically, but practically. You'll see how **money tests your values**, exposes your psychological weaknesses, and reveals the ethical foundation (or fragility) beneath your ambition. We'll unpack how **integrity compounds faster than capital** when aligned with purpose, and how the true measure of wealth lies not in assets, but in the harmony between one's **decisions, ethics, and time horizon**.

Ultimately, the goal isn't to moralize wealth it's to understand it as an **extension of self-mastery**. When you trade with integrity, patience, and principle, money becomes not a mirror of greed, but a reflection of growth and your financial journey transforms into a moral and psychological evolution in itself.

19.1 Wealth Amplifies Personality

Wealth is often mistaken for transformation as if the acquisition of money could somehow alter the essence of a person. In truth, wealth does not change people; it **amplifies** who they already are. It functions as a psychological loudspeaker, projecting one's inner character onto a larger stage. The generous become more giving. The insecure seek validation through excess. The disciplined build empires quietly, while the reckless multiply their self-destructive tendencies at scale.

In the markets, this amplification is accelerated by leverage both financial and emotional. When traders suddenly profit beyond their expectations, their underlying traits surge to the surface. The humble see their gain as evidence of discipline and luck intertwined. The arrogant interpret it as proof of superiority. The fearful, even when successful, find new anxieties to obsess over. In this way, *money does not rewrite personality; it reveals it under pressure and prosperity alike.*

The relationship between wealth and personality can be framed as a psychological equation:

$$\text{Amplified Behavior} = \text{Core Trait} \times \text{Financial Magnitude}$$

If the core trait is insecurity, then more money means larger displays of overcompensation expensive distractions that signal worth rather than embody it. If the core trait is curiosity, wealth funds exploration, education, and innovation. Thus, every dollar earned becomes a reflection of one's internal architecture. The market rewards or punishes not just skill, but the mindset behind it.

History offers endless examples. Consider the investor who, after a lucky run, expands risk recklessly driven not by opportunity but by ego. Or the disciplined allocator who compounds patiently, unmoved by others' success, because their relationship with money is rooted in stewardship, not status. In both cases, wealth amplifies the inner truth. It is a mirror that magnifies not just capability, but **character under abundance.**

This amplification also extends to morality. When resources grow, so does the capacity to do both good and harm. A small ethical flaw, when paired with vast capital, can influence entire systems. Conversely, integrity combined with wealth can uplift communities, fund innovation, and create enduring value. The moral weight of wealth thus depends not on its quantity, but on the **quality of the person who wields it.**

Ultimately, understanding that wealth amplifies personality invites introspection. Before seeking to increase capital, one must clarify: *What part of myself will be multiplied if I succeed?* Because every profitable decision, every compounding return, scales not only your portfolio it scales your habits, fears, and moral compass. Without self-awareness, success becomes a spotlight that blinds rather than illuminates. With it, wealth becomes a tool for expansion not of ego, but of conscious purpose.

19.2 Moral Dimensions of Profit-Seeking

Profit-seeking is the heartbeat of all markets the primal motive that drives innovation, competition, and human progress. Yet, beneath its economic logic lies an ethical landscape rarely examined with the same rigor as financial analysis. To seek profit is not merely to allocate capital; it is to navigate a moral terrain where intention, consequence, and integrity constantly intersect.

At its core, the pursuit of profit raises a fundamental question: *At what cost?* This question is not purely financial it is psychological and philosophical. Every trade, investment, or business decision represents a moral choice about value creation versus extraction, contribution versus exploitation. In other words, **profit is never ethically neutral.** It either reflects alignment with long-term societal value or a short-term indulgence in opportunism.

The moral dimension becomes more visible when we recognize that profit operates as a social signal. Markets are collective moral systems disguised as price mechanisms. Prices encode not only scarcity and demand but also the values of those participating. When speculation rewards manipulation, the system's moral compass tilts. When innovation rewards genuine utility, integrity becomes profitable. Thus, the structure of incentives determines whether markets evolve as engines of progress or amplifiers of greed.

From a behavioral perspective, the drive for profit often blurs ethical clarity. Cognitive biases such as moral licensing, self-serving rationalization, and outcome bias enable traders and investors to justify questionable behavior as "just part of the game." For instance, insider information, deceptive marketing, or predatory pricing are often rationalized as competitive advantages rather than moral violations. The mind's need to preserve self-image constructs narratives that make unethical actions appear logical or even necessary.

Philosophically, profit-seeking can be viewed along a spectrum. On one end lies the **extractive mindset** profit derived by exploiting inefficiencies, human weakness, or information asymmetry without adding enduring value. On the other end lies the **constructive mindset** profit as a byproduct of solving real problems, creating innovation, and improving collective welfare.

Both may generate monetary gain, but only the latter compounds reputational and ethical capital. Over time, markets punish unethical asymmetry through regulation, social backlash, or loss of trust even if delayed.

Historically, every financial bubble and crash has reflected this moral tension. During booms, ethical vigilance weakens under collective euphoria; in crashes, society reasserts moral order through reform. The 2008 financial crisis, for example, was not only a failure of risk management but also a failure of moral responsibility the systematic prioritization of short-term gain over structural stability. Similarly, speculative manias in cryptocurrencies or AI stocks often echo the same pattern: moral caution drowned by the promise of exponential return.

Ethically aware traders and investors recognize that **profit and principle are not opposites but partners in sustainability.** Integrity acts as invisible alpha compounding quietly through reputation, trust, and consistency. While markets may reward questionable tactics in the short term, long-term compounding favors those whose pursuit of profit aligns with transparency, fairness, and genuine value creation. As in life, the market eventually prices in character.

Therefore, the moral dimension of profit-seeking is not about moralizing capitalism, but about understanding that markets mirror the collective ethics of their participants. Every portfolio, every trading decision, is a moral artifact a reflection of how one defines "enough," and what one is willing to compromise to reach it. The most evolved traders and investors understand that ethical restraint is not weakness but strength a stabilizing force that prevents self-destruction masked as ambition.

In the end, profit is not simply what remains after expenses. It is what remains of your integrity after success.

19.3 Ethical Asymmetry: Decision × Integrity × Time = Legacy

In markets as in life asymmetry defines everything. Traders hunt for asymmetric opportunities: small risks with the potential for large rewards. But beyond financial asymmetry lies a deeper, often ignored dimension **ethical asymmetry**. It is the unseen compounder that determines not just who wins, but who endures.

Ethical asymmetry can be expressed as a simple equation:

$$\text{Legacy} = \text{Decision} \times \text{Integrity} \times \text{Time}$$

This formula reframes how we think about success. Every decision has a magnitude (its impact), integrity gives it direction (its moral vector), and time compounds both. Just as interest magnifies capital, integrity magnifies consequence. Without integrity, even the most brilliant decision eventually self-destructs; with it, even modest actions can resonate across decades.

In the short run, unethical behavior often looks efficient it accelerates results, wins deals, and inflates returns. But in the long run, it introduces hidden risk: reputational decay, loss of trust, and internal dissonance. These moral liabilities do not appear on balance sheets, yet they determine the sustainability of every fortune and every career. Ethical asymmetry reminds us that markets are not just pricing mechanisms they are moral echo chambers. Every action reverberates through time, returning amplified consequences to its source.

Integrity, therefore, is not an abstract virtue but an asset class a form of invisible equity that compounds silently in the background. The trader who acts with consistency, transparency, and restraint builds credibility that outlasts any single market cycle. Over time, this credibility becomes legacy the ultimate asymmetrical payoff: finite effort, infinite memory.

Ethical asymmetry is what separates transient success from enduring significance. It transforms wealth from accumulation into meaning. In the end, what survives the chart, the trade, or the profit statement is not what you gained but how you gained it.

Chapter 20

The Social Side of Money

Money, at its core, is a social construct a shared story that binds human cooperation. Yet beneath its practical function as a medium of exchange lies something far more primal: status. We don't merely earn money to survive; we earn it to be seen, valued, and respected. Every salary, portfolio, and luxury purchase is part of an invisible social dialogue a continuous negotiation of rank within the tribe.

The markets, too, are not just arenas of price discovery but of identity discovery. Traders compete not only for profits but for validation the thrill of being right, the prestige of foresight, the dopamine of recognition. Behind every bold trade or investment is a subtle social motive: to prove oneself superior, smarter, or more deserving than the crowd.

This chapter explores how the pursuit of wealth intertwines with the pursuit of status. It dissects the invisible games of envy, comparison, and imitation that shape financial decisions far more than spreadsheets or models ever do. Because, in truth, people rarely want money itself they want what it symbolizes: relative success.

Through behavioral economics, evolutionary psychology, and real-world examples, we will examine how social proof drives bubbles, how envy fuels risk-taking, and how comparison traps can destroy both peace and portfolio. Understanding the social dynamics of money reveals a paradox that our greatest financial struggles often stem not from scarcity of capital, but from the endless need to look richer than others.

In mastering markets, then, one must first master the ego's social cravings. The illusion of comparison is the modern trader's mirage: a chase that promises satisfaction yet delivers perpetual dissatisfaction. Recognizing this truth frees us to view money not as a mirror of our worth, but as a neutral tool one that can serve wisdom as easily as it can serve vanity.

20.1 Status Games, Envy, and Social Proof

At the heart of every financial system lies a silent, ancient force the human desire for status. Money, in its purest form, was designed to measure value. But in modern society, it has evolved into something more a scoreboard of self-worth. We no longer seek money merely to buy comfort or security; we seek it to buy distinction. The accumulation of wealth becomes a symbolic way to declare, "I matter more than others."

This psychological game of status is as old as civilization itself. In tribal societies, status was conferred through hunting success, wisdom, or strength. In the modern financial tribe, status manifests through visible wealth the house in the right neighborhood, the luxury car, the portfolio screenshot, the exclusive investment opportunity. Every market bubble, from tulips to tech stocks, is in part a collective display of this primal need for recognition and belonging.

The Status Game Loop

Status is inherently relative. It does not exist in isolation; it thrives in comparison. A person earning $1 million a year may feel poor if surrounded by billionaires, yet rich if surrounded by the middle class. The mind, designed for survival in small tribes, still compares within its social circle. In the digital era, that circle has expanded to billions amplifying envy, inadequacy, and the need to signal success.

This creates the status game loop:

1. We observe others' visible success (social proof).
2. We feel internal envy or inadequacy.
3. We take financial action often impulsively to "catch up."
4. We signal success publicly, restarting the cycle for someone else.

Social media has weaponized this loop. Platforms like Instagram, X (Twitter), and YouTube have transformed wealth into theater where perception often outweighs reality. Traders show profits, not losses. Influencers flaunt luxury, not debt. Investors broadcast wins, not risks. The subconscious result: a distorted belief that everyone else is succeeding faster, pushing individuals toward riskier, emotionally-driven decisions.

Envy: The Hidden Fuel of Markets

Envy is one of the least acknowledged yet most potent emotional drivers in finance. It is envy that makes investors chase parabolic rallies, buy overvalued assets, or refuse to sell at rational points. When someone else's success is visible, the human brain interprets it as a loss of social rank. We are wired to close that gap not through logic, but through action. This is why the late stage of every bull market is dominated not by analysis but by emotion a mass psychological effort to avoid "being left behind."

In evolutionary terms, envy was adaptive; it motivated individuals to improve their standing within the tribe. But in markets, it becomes destructive. The pursuit of relative gain often leads to absolute loss. As Warren Buffett famously observed, "It's not greed that drives the world, but envy." Markets oscillate because emotions oscillate and envy is one of the strongest of all oscillators.

Social Proof: The Comfort of the Crowd

Humans are social learners. In uncertain environments like markets the brain looks to others for cues. This is the principle of social proof: when we see others acting confidently, we assume they possess information we don't. During bubbles, this effect compounds; as prices rise, the crowd's conviction appears to validate itself. The fear of missing out (FOMO) then merges with the illusion of certainty.

Social proof can create temporary stability as in coordinated institutional flows but also catastrophic fragility. When the same herd that bought on euphoria rushes to exit in fear, liquidity vanishes and panic ensues. Understanding social proof means recognizing that the crowd is not always irrational it's simply emotional in the same direction at the same time.

Escaping the Status Trap

To play the market well, one must step outside the social game. True financial mastery begins when the scoreboard shifts from "better than others" to "better than yesterday." Internal metrics discipline, process, risk control must replace external validation. The wealthiest traders in spirit are not those who win the most trades, but those who are least controlled by envy and comparison.

Freedom in markets, and in life, emerges when you no longer play games you didn't choose. Money should serve as a mirror for self-knowledge, not as a mask for self-worth. When status, envy, and social proof lose their hold, rationality returns and so does peace.

20.2 Why People Don't Want Money They Want Relative Success

Money is a means, not an end. What most people actually pursue is a position in a social hierarchy a sense that they are doing better than others, or at least better than they used to. That distinction *relative success* versus absolute wealth is the invisible engine behind many financial decisions, from lifestyle inflation to speculative risk-taking. This section explains why relative position matters psychologically, how it shapes economic behavior, and what traders and investors should know about its market consequences.

The Psychology of Relative Success

Humans evolved in small groups where rank determined access to mates, allies, and resources. Although modern societies are vastly different, the psychology that prized relative standing remains intact:

- **Social comparison:** People evaluate their own outcomes by comparing them with peers. Income, possessions, and visible signs of success become yardsticks for self-worth.
- **Status as signal:** Wealth serves as a public signal a fast and easily observed indicator of competence, power, or belonging. Signaling theory explains why visible consumption often outweighs quiet savings: public signals change social perception quickly.
- **Rank over level:** Research and everyday experience show that subjective well-being correlates strongly with relative rank (how you stand against others) rather than absolute level (how much you physically own). A small step up the social ladder can feel larger than a big increase that leaves your relative position unchanged.

These drivers explain why people prefer a smaller slice of a larger pie when it improves their rank, rather than an objectively larger pie that leaves their relative position unchanged.

Economic and Behavioral Consequences

The preference for relative success produces predictable behaviors that ripple across markets and personal finance:

- **Conspicuous consumption:** Spending on visible goods (cars, watches, homes) increases because public display shifts perceived rank faster than private goods.
- **Keeping up with the Joneses:** Consumption choices are often driven by local reference groups; neighborhood, workplace, and social feeds create potent, shifting benchmarks.
- **Status inflation:** As standards of visible success rise, people spend more to maintain the same relative status (a modern hedonic treadmill).
- **Risk-taking for reputation:** Individuals (and managers) sometimes take outsized risks to achieve dramatic wins that enhance reputation even when those risks lower long-term expected utility.

- **Market-level effects:** When many participants chase relative gains or visible success, flows concentrate, volatility rises, and bubbles become more likely as status-seeking amplifies momentum.

How Relative Success Drives Market Behavior

Relative motives influence markets in concrete ways:

- **Herding and momentum:** Seeing peers profit creates social proof; those seeking relative success pile into the same trades, reinforcing trends.
- **Performance pressure:** Fund managers and professionals face career risk tied to relative performance (rank versus peers), which can encourage herding, benchmark-chasing, and short-termism.
- **Visibility-driven bubbles:** New asset classes that provide public success stories (home equity, crypto, tech IPOs) attract status-driven capital quickly, raising the odds of excess valuation.

Understanding these mechanisms helps explain why markets often move for social reasons more than for marginal changes in fundamentals.

The Inner Cost of Comparison

Pursuing relative success carries hidden costs that erode long-term well-being and financial stability:

- **Emotional volatility:** Tying self-worth to others' outcomes creates chronic anxiety and dissatisfaction success is never stable because reference groups change.
- **Suboptimal decisions:** Choices optimized for outward appearance (status) are frequently suboptimal for long-term wealth accumulation (overconsumption, high leverage).
- **Reputational risk:** Chasing visible wins can lead to ethical shortcuts or reckless bets that damage reputation the one form of capital that compounds like interest over decades.

Practical Strategies to Escape the Comparison Trap

Because relative motives are powerful and often unconscious, deliberate practices are required to counteract them. The following tools help align financial action with genuine goals rather than status pressures:

1. **Define intrinsic metrics:** Replace external benchmarks with internal ones (e.g., percent savings rate, risk-adjusted return targets, progress toward personal goals). Measure yourself against yesterday, not your neighbor.

2. **Visibility thermostat:** Reduce public sharing of financial wins (and consumption). Social media and public displays amplify status signals; control the thermostat by limiting exposure.

3. **The "If nobody saw it" test:** Before making any purchase or leverage decision, ask: "Would I still make this choice if nobody in my social circle knew about it?" If the answer is no, the action is likely status-driven.

4. **Commitment devices:** Use rules, auto-savings, and binding decisions to guard against impulse spending aimed at signaling. Precommitment neutralizes short-term status impulses.

5. **Phased visibility:** If signaling is useful (business, networking), do it strategically and intentionally; otherwise keep wealth accumulation private to avoid socially induced escalation.

6. **Cultivate non-material status:** Invest in reputation, competence, and relationships forms of status that compound without forcing conspicuous consumption.

Implications for Traders and Investors

For market participants, awareness of relative motives leads to better decisions:

- Recognize when your trade is motivated by the desire to "beat the benchmark" rather than by asymmetric edge.
- Beware of career-risk-driven performance chases that push you into crowded trades; structure incentives and size to align with long-term edge, not short-term rank.
- Use private metrics to evaluate performance; public bragging or comparison often distorts risk-taking.

Key Insight

Most people do not want money for its own sake they want the social rewards it brings. Because those rewards are relative, they drive behaviors (consumption, risk-taking, signaling) that can undermine both well-being and financial prudence. By recognizing the distinction between absolute wealth and relative success, and by designing personal systems that privilege intrinsic metrics and slow compounding of integrity and competence, you insulate yourself from the corrosive effects of comparison and turn money back into a tool rather than a mirror for insecurity.

20.3 The Illusion of Comparison

Comparison is one of the most persistent and powerful psychological forces driving human behavior and in finance, it is often an illusion. The mind constantly evaluates outcomes relative to peers, neighbors, and reference groups, creating a perception of scarcity or inadequacy that may not actually exist. This illusion warps decision-making, fuels risk-taking, and distorts our perception of success.

Why Comparison Feels Real

The human brain evolved to operate in social groups, where relative status determined access to resources, mates, and protection. In modern markets, this instinct is misapplied: instead of small-group survival, we are exposed to billions of peers via social media, news, and public wealth displays. The comparison instinct interprets these signals as directly relevant to personal survival or status, even when they are largely irrelevant.

- **Anchoring to external signals:** We anchor to the visible success of others their portfolio gains, lifestyle, or job achievements and unconsciously treat them as a standard we must match or exceed.
- **Relative deprivation:** Even when absolute wealth or performance is strong, seeing others achieve more triggers feelings of loss or inadequacy. The gap is often imaginary, exaggerated, or temporary, yet it drives real emotional reactions.
- **Social amplification:** Online feeds and media amplify the illusion, selectively showcasing peaks of success and hiding failures. This curated reality magnifies envy, fear of missing out (FOMO), and impulsive behavior.

Market Consequences of Illusory Comparison

The illusion of comparison shapes collective behavior, often creating cycles of overconfidence, herd behavior, and bubbles:

- **Chasing visible winners:** Investors may pile into assets simply because peers are profiting, regardless of underlying fundamentals.
- **Over-leveraging to match peers:** Traders often take outsized positions to "keep up," increasing systemic risk and personal exposure.
- **Perpetual dissatisfaction:** No matter how much one earns or gains, comparison ensures the feeling of inadequacy persists, driving continuous risk-seeking behavior.

Breaking Free from the Illusion

The first step is recognizing that comparison is a mental construct, not a reflection of reality. Practical strategies include:

1. **Shift to absolute metrics:** Track your performance using intrinsic benchmarks (growth, risk-adjusted returns, personal improvement) rather than relative rankings.
2. **Limit exposure to curated success:** Reduce time spent on social media, finance forums, or newsletters that showcase selective gains.
3. **Practice reflective evaluation:** Before reacting to another's success, ask: "Does this truly impact my strategy or my goals?"
4. **Embrace process over outcomes:** Focus on decisions and discipline rather than ephemeral results or external validation.

Key Insight

The comparison trap is an illusion magnified by social signals and cognitive biases. Markets are not just arenas of financial exchange; they are mirrors reflecting our social instincts back at us. By recognizing the distortion, privileging intrinsic metrics, and aligning decisions with personal goals rather than peer benchmarks, one can regain rationality, reduce emotional volatility, and reclaim agency over financial and personal well-being.

Chapter 21

The Emotional Cost of Success

Success in markets and in life is often celebrated as the ultimate goal. Profits, recognition, and status are visible, quantifiable, and widely admired. Yet beneath the surface of every achievement lies a hidden toll the emotional cost of pursuing and maintaining success. While victories are visible, the psychological strain, isolation, and relentless pressure that accompany them remain largely unspoken.

Traders, investors, and high performers often operate in environments of intense scrutiny, self-imposed expectations, and constant uncertainty. The same traits that drive exceptional performance discipline, focus, ambition can also create vulnerability to burnout, obsession, and loneliness. Paradoxically, the very qualities that enable high achievement can amplify the emotional weight of success.

This chapter explores the psychological and emotional dimensions of sustained performance. We will examine the pressures of continuous success, the isolation that often accompanies exceptional results, and the challenges of finding fulfillment beyond wins. By understanding the hidden costs, readers can develop strategies to sustain both financial achievement and mental well-being, ensuring that success becomes a source of enrichment rather than a trigger for stress and imbalance.

In essence, mastering markets is not only about managing risk, analyzing trends, or exploiting asymmetry it is also about managing the self. Emotional resilience, self-awareness, and the ability to find meaning beyond mere profits are critical to long-term fulfillment and sustainable success.

21.1 Burnout, Obsession, Isolation

Success in trading and investing often demands extreme focus, long hours, and high mental energy. While these traits can produce extraordinary results, they come with significant emotional and psychological costs. Burnout, obsession, and isolation are common, yet frequently unrecognized, consequences of sustained high performance.

Burnout: The Hidden Drag on Performance

Burnout is a state of chronic physical and emotional exhaustion, often accompanied by reduced motivation and cognitive decline. In financial markets, burnout can emerge from:

- **Relentless decision-making:** Markets operate 24/7, and high performers constantly analyze, strategize, and execute trades. The cumulative cognitive load can lead to mental fatigue.
- **Emotional volatility:** Frequent exposure to gains and losses, fear, and pressure to outperform peers triggers chronic stress responses in the brain, wearing down resilience over time.
- **Lack of recovery:** Ignoring rest, sleep, and downtime prevents neural and emotional recovery, reducing clarity and increasing impulsivity.

Burnout not only impairs decision-making but can also manifest physically with sleep disturbances, weakened immunity, and cardiovascular strain creating a feedback loop that further reduces performance.

Obsession: The Double-Edged Sword

Obsessive focus can be a key differentiator between average and elite performers, but it also carries risks:

- **Tunnel vision:** Excessive attention to markets or performance metrics can narrow perspective, causing traders to ignore warning signals or alternative opportunities.
- **Identity fusion:** When one's self-worth becomes inseparable from trading success, every loss feels catastrophic, amplifying stress and anxiety.
- **Compulsive behaviors:** Obsession can lead to overtrading, revenge trading, and rigid adherence to strategies without contextual flexibility.

The very intensity that enables mastery can thus morph into a liability if left unmanaged.

Isolation: The Loneliness of Consistent Performers

High achievers often operate in solitude, whether by choice or necessity:

- **Social disconnect:** Long hours and hyper-focus can reduce time spent with family, friends, and supportive networks.
- **Peer scarcity:** Few can relate to the pressures of consistently high performance, creating a sense of alienation.
- **Emotional bottling:** Discussing stress or doubt may feel risky or unnecessary, reinforcing isolation and reducing opportunities for perspective or advice.

Isolation compounds burnout and obsession, forming a cycle where high performance carries invisible emotional costs.

Practical Strategies for Mitigation

To sustain success without sacrificing mental health, consider the following:

1. **Scheduled recovery:** Allocate consistent time for rest, exercise, and hobbies that disengage the mind from markets.
2. **Boundary setting:** Define limits on trading hours, screen time, and emotional engagement with outcomes.
3. **Emotional self-awareness:** Regularly track stress, fatigue, and obsessive patterns in a journal or reflection log.
4. **Support networks:** Maintain relationships with peers, mentors, and friends who can provide perspective, encouragement, and grounding.
5. **Purpose beyond profit:** Cultivate goals and activities that generate intrinsic satisfaction outside financial results learning, giving, creativity, or community impact.

Key Insight

> *Success is not measured solely by wins or wealth, but by the ability to sustain high performance without sacrificing emotional and physical well-being. Burnout, obsession, and isolation are the hidden taxes of achievement. Recognizing and mitigating these forces transforms success from a fleeting reward into a sustainable, fulfilling journey.*

21.2 Loneliness of Consistent Performers

Consistent high performance in markets, investing, or trading often comes with a hidden companion: loneliness. While skill, discipline, and strategic insight drive repeated success, they also set the performer apart from peers, colleagues, and social networks. Loneliness is not merely a social inconvenience; it has profound psychological and behavioral implications that can affect decision-making, risk tolerance, and long-term well-being.

Why Loneliness Occurs

Several factors contribute to the isolation of consistent performers:

- **Rarity of peers:** Individuals who consistently succeed in high-stakes domains are few. With limited peers who truly understand the pressures, it can be difficult to find relatable advice or support.
- **Self-imposed boundaries:** Maintaining focus, avoiding distractions, and dedicating extensive hours to work can limit social interactions, deepening feelings of isolation.
- **Perceived competition:** Even among peers, competitive dynamics can inhibit vulnerability. Sharing doubts, fears, or mistakes may feel risky if others could capitalize on them.
- **Identity fusion:** When self-worth is tied to success, performers may avoid discussing personal challenges, fearing that it undermines credibility or status.

Psychological and Behavioral Impacts

The loneliness experienced by high performers has tangible effects on the mind and behavior:

- **Increased stress and anxiety:** Lack of social support amplifies stress responses to market fluctuations, mistakes, or unforeseen outcomes.
- **Cognitive biases intensify:** Without external perspectives, confirmation bias, overconfidence, and emotional reasoning can dominate decision-making.
- **Emotional fatigue:** The burden of managing performance pressures alone leads to mental exhaustion, reducing the ability to respond adaptively to new information.
- **Risk distortion:** Loneliness can push individuals toward either excessive risk-taking to prove capability or extreme risk aversion to avoid failure in isolation.

Breaking the Isolation Loop

While some degree of solitude is necessary for focus and mastery, deliberate strategies can mitigate the negative aspects of loneliness:

1. **Cultivate a support network:** Engage with mentors, peers, or communities who understand market dynamics and can provide feedback without judgment.
2. **Structured peer interaction:** Regularly participate in study groups, trading circles, or discussion forums to maintain connection and perspective.
3. **Transparency with self:** Keep a reflective journal to articulate thoughts, fears, and insights, creating an internal dialogue even when external conversation is limited.
4. **Balanced social life:** Prioritize relationships outside the market friends, family, hobbies to anchor identity and emotional health beyond performance metrics.
5. **Professional guidance:** Engage coaches, psychologists, or behavioral finance specialists to help navigate the emotional landscape of consistent high performance.

Key Insight

Consistency in performance often comes at the cost of connection. Loneliness magnifies stress, biases, and emotional fatigue, subtly undermining both decision-making and well-being. By intentionally cultivating support networks, maintaining reflective practices, and separating identity from outcomes, high performers can preserve both their edge and their mental health, transforming solitude into a tool for clarity rather than a trap of isolation.

21.3 Finding Meaning Beyond Wins

While financial success, trading victories, and market mastery are tangible measures of achievement, they often provide only fleeting satisfaction. The human mind seeks purpose, fulfillment, and significance beyond numbers and charts. Without this deeper sense of meaning, even the most impressive wins can feel hollow, leading to emotional fatigue, obsession, or a constant need for validation.

The Limits of External Success

External achievements profits, accolades, or status are inherently unstable:

- **Ephemeral rewards:** Market gains are temporary and can fluctuate with every session, creating a roller-coaster of emotions tied to outcomes rather than effort or skill.
- **Comparison traps:** Success is often evaluated relative to others, rather than on personal growth or long-term objectives, perpetuating the illusion of inadequacy.
- **Hedonic adaptation:** Humans quickly acclimate to achievements; the thrill of a big win diminishes over time, leaving a craving for the next accomplishment without lasting fulfillment.

Purpose as a Stabilizer

Finding meaning beyond wins requires connecting actions to intrinsic values and long-term purpose:

- **Align with personal values:** Identify what truly matters whether it's mastery, learning, contribution, or growth and use it as the benchmark for success.
- **Focus on process over outcome:** Shift attention from individual wins to disciplined execution, strategy development, and the refinement of skills. The journey becomes the reward.
- **Contribute beyond self:** Use financial gains, expertise, or influence to support others, mentor, or create impact. Giving creates a deeper sense of fulfillment than accumulation alone.

Psychological and Emotional Benefits

When success is tied to meaningful purpose rather than purely external outcomes:

- **Resilience increases:** Setbacks and losses are interpreted as part of the learning and growth process, not as existential failures.
- **Stress diminishes:** Emotional attachment to volatile market results decreases, improving decision-making and mental clarity.
- **Sustainable motivation:** Engagement with work or trading is driven by values and curiosity rather than fleeting reward cycles, creating longevity in performance.

Practical Strategies for Meaningful Success

1. **Reflect regularly:** Schedule weekly or monthly sessions to evaluate whether actions and goals align with personal values.

2. **Set process-oriented goals:** Define success in terms of behaviors, learning, or skill refinement rather than purely financial outcomes.
3. **Balance work and life:** Integrate activities that provide joy, connection, and growth outside the market.
4. **Mentorship and contribution:** Share knowledge, support others, and participate in communities to amplify purpose beyond self-interest.
5. **Practice gratitude:** Focus on achievements, growth, and opportunities, cultivating contentment and psychological well-being.

Key Insight

True mastery and lasting satisfaction in markets or in life arise not from the wins themselves, but from the meaning attached to them. By grounding actions in purpose, valuing the process over outcomes, and extending impact beyond oneself, success transforms from a fleeting triumph into enduring fulfillment. Financial gains become a tool, not a measure, of a life well-lived.

Chapter 22

The Paradox of Control

In trading, investing, and life, there is a fundamental tension between effort and outcome: the more we try to control results, the more we expose ourselves to frustration, stress, and error. Markets are inherently uncertain, influenced by countless variables beyond any single individual's control. Yet, humans are wired to seek mastery through control, often mistaking effort and activity for influence over outcomes.

This chapter explores the paradox of control: while we cannot dictate market movements or guarantee success, we can manage our exposure, mindset, and decision-making process. True mastery is not about predicting every twist of the market, but about cultivating resilience, emotional equilibrium, and strategic discernment. By letting go of illusory control, traders and investors can achieve clarity, reduce anxiety, and make decisions rooted in probability and process rather than fear or ego.

We will examine strategies for accepting uncertainty, focusing on controllable factors, and transforming the act of letting go into a form of strength. Through reflection and disciplined awareness, it is possible to navigate volatility with serenity, aligning actions with purpose rather than attachment to outcomes.

Ultimately, this chapter reveals that control is not the opposite of uncertainty it is the intelligent management of exposure, perception, and choice within an uncertain world.

22.1 You Can't Control Outcomes, Only Exposure

One of the most profound lessons in trading, investing, and decision-making is that outcomes are never fully within our control. No matter how skilled or disciplined a trader becomes, external factors market sentiment, geopolitical events, macroeconomic shifts, and even random chance can alter results in ways that are impossible to predict. Attempting to control these outcomes leads to stress, frustration, and often poor decision-making.

Instead, mastery lies in controlling what is actually within our influence: our exposure. Exposure refers to the degree of risk, engagement, and responsibility we take on in any given situation. By managing exposure, we create conditions where we can perform optimally without being emotionally or financially overleveraged. This concept reframes control from a futile attempt to dictate the future to a practical, actionable strategy for survival and growth in uncertain environments.

Understanding Exposure

Exposure is multidimensional and includes:

- **Financial Exposure:** Position sizing, leverage, and allocation of capital that determines the magnitude of potential gain or loss.
- **Emotional Exposure:** The degree to which outcomes affect mental states, confidence, and behavioral responses. High emotional exposure can lead to impulsive decisions and burnout.
- **Temporal Exposure:** The length of time we remain committed to a particular trade, investment, or decision path, which affects both risk and stress.
- **Cognitive Exposure:** The degree to which we tie our identity or self-worth to outcomes, magnifying the psychological stakes of every result.

Why Outcomes Cannot Be Controlled

Markets are a complex system of interacting participants, news flows, and feedback loops. Even the most sophisticated models cannot perfectly predict future price movements. Attempting to force control leads to common pitfalls:

- **Overtrading:** Trying to react to every market fluctuation increases transaction costs and emotional stress.
- **Confirmation Bias:** Seeking only information that supports your expected outcome can blind you to reality.
- **Illusion of Control:** Overestimating the influence of personal skill on random or collective outcomes leads to reckless risk-taking.

Managing Exposure for Mastery

Effective management of exposure allows individuals to navigate uncertainty while preserving both capital and composure:

1. **Define risk boundaries:** Set clear financial limits on any position relative to your portfolio and risk tolerance.
2. **Detach ego from results:** Recognize that losses or setbacks do not define your skill or worth.
3. **Embrace probabilistic thinking:** Focus on expected outcomes and likelihoods rather than certainty.
4. **Diversify exposure:** Spread financial, emotional, and cognitive risks across strategies, timeframes, and assets to reduce vulnerability.
5. **Reflect and adjust:** Regularly evaluate exposure levels and refine strategies to maintain balance and resilience.

Key Insight

Control is an illusion when it comes to outcomes, but exposure is tangible and actionable. By consciously managing what you put at stake financially, emotionally, and cognitively you can navigate uncertainty with clarity, reduce stress, and increase the probability of long-term success. Mastery is not forcing the market to comply; it is mastering yourself in the face of unpredictability.

22.2 Letting Go as Mastery

In trading, investing, and decision-making, one of the most counterintuitive yet powerful forms of mastery is learning to let go. Letting go does not mean passivity or inaction; rather, it is the deliberate release of attachment to specific outcomes, the surrender of the illusion that we can control everything, and the conscious focus on what is within our influence. This mental shift transforms stress into clarity, fear into discipline, and impulsive reactions into rational decision-making.

The Burden of Attachment

Attachment to outcomes is a fundamental source of stress and emotional turbulence:

- **Emotional volatility:** When we tie our identity or self-worth to every trade or investment, every fluctuation triggers anxiety, overreaction, or panic.

- **Impaired judgment:** Strong attachment fosters impulsivity, over-trading, and the inability to cut losses or exit underperforming positions.
- **Cognitive distortion:** Attachment magnifies biases like confirmation, recency, and hindsight, leading to systematic errors in judgment.

Recognizing that attachment amplifies risk is the first step toward mastery.

The Psychology of Letting Go

Letting go involves shifting from outcome-based thinking to process-oriented thinking:

- **Focus on controllable factors:** Concentrate on preparation, research, risk management, and execution rather than obsessing over market responses.
- **Accept uncertainty:** Embrace the reality that markets are unpredictable, and that losses or setbacks are a natural component of probabilistic systems.
- **Reframe success and failure:** View every outcome as information, feedback, or learning, rather than as a personal judgment or measure of worth.

Neuroscience confirms that the brain responds to attachment with heightened stress signals, while detachment allows rational, prefrontal cortex-mediated decision-making to dominate over emotional impulses.

Practical Strategies for Letting Go

1. **Predefine rules and limits:** Establish clear entry, exit, and position-sizing rules so decisions are guided by process rather than emotion.
2. **Use journaling and reflection:** Record trades, decisions, and emotional reactions to recognize patterns of attachment and bias.
3. **Mindfulness and meditation:** Practice observing thoughts and emotions without judgment, training the mind to release fixation on outcomes.
4. **Focus on probability:** Think in terms of likelihoods and ranges rather than absolutes, accepting that no strategy guarantees a specific result.
5. **Detach identity from performance:** Separate self-worth from success or failure, reinforcing that setbacks are opportunities for growth, not personal flaws.

The Power of Letting Go

Letting go is not surrendering control over your actions it is mastering control over your responses. When you release attachment to outcomes:

- Emotional clarity increases, allowing for more rational decisions.
- Patience improves, enabling you to wait for asymmetric opportunities.
- Stress diminishes, protecting both mental and physical well-being.
- Long-term consistency and resilience rise, as performance is guided by disciplined process rather than short-term emotion.

Key Insight

> *Mastery lies not in forcing the market to conform to your desires, but in aligning your mind with the reality of uncertainty. By letting go of attachment to specific outcomes, you transform vulnerability into clarity, fear into disciplined action, and volatility into opportunity. True control is found in your response, not in the results.*

22.3 Serenity in Uncertainty

Uncertainty is an inescapable reality in markets, investing, and life. Prices fluctuate, news shifts, and external events unfold in unpredictable ways. Attempting to eliminate uncertainty is both impossible and counterproductive. Serenity in uncertainty, however, is a skill a state of mental calm and clarity that allows individuals to act decisively and rationally despite the unknown.

The Nature of Uncertainty

Uncertainty arises because markets are complex adaptive systems, influenced by countless interconnected factors:

- **Information asymmetry:** No single participant has access to all information, and perceptions differ widely.
- **Human behavior:** Collective psychology, emotions, and biases drive irrational swings that defy purely logical predictions.
- **Randomness and chance:** Even with perfect analysis, unpredictable events can alter outcomes.

Understanding that uncertainty is inherent rather than exceptional is the first step toward achieving serenity.

Psychological Impacts of Uncertainty

Uncertainty can trigger stress responses, fear, and reactive behaviors:

- **Anxiety and overtrading:** Fear of missing out or fear of loss can lead to impulsive actions.
- **Paralysis by analysis:** Overthinking and seeking certainty can delay decision-making, missing opportunities.
- **Emotional bias:** Ambiguity often amplifies cognitive biases, such as overconfidence or loss aversion.

Without strategies to manage these responses, uncertainty can become a source of chronic stress rather than a navigable condition.

Cultivating Serenity

Serenity in uncertainty is cultivated through mindset, discipline, and practice:

1. **Focus on process, not outcome:** Concentrate on preparation, execution, and risk management the aspects you can control.
2. **Probabilistic thinking:** Evaluate scenarios in terms of likelihoods and ranges rather than certainties, accepting both success and failure as part of a broader distribution of outcomes.
3. **Mindfulness and emotional regulation:** Practice observing thoughts and emotions without judgment, reducing reactivity to market fluctuations.
4. **Flexible adaptation:** Be prepared to adjust strategies as new information emerges, rather than clinging rigidly to preconceived notions.
5. **Reflective practice:** Regularly assess what drives your decisions profit, ego, or purpose and recalibrate your approach to align with long-term goals.

Benefits of Serenity in Uncertainty

Achieving serenity in uncertainty yields profound advantages:

- **Improved decision-making:** Calm minds process information more effectively and avoid impulsive choices.
- **Emotional resilience:** Reduced stress and fear enhance long-term mental and physical health.
- **Consistency and longevity:** Traders and investors who maintain serenity are more likely to remain disciplined, adapt, and thrive across market cycles.

- **Clarity and insight:** By reducing emotional noise, one can recognize patterns, opportunities, and risks with greater precision.

Key Insight

Uncertainty is inevitable, but panic is optional. Serenity in uncertainty is the hallmark of mastery a state where fear does not dictate action, and clarity guides strategy. By focusing on controllable factors, thinking probabilistically, and embracing adaptability, one can transform uncertainty from a source of anxiety into a catalyst for disciplined opportunity.

Actionable Insight: Reflect Weekly on What Drives Your Decisions Profit, Ego, or Purpose

Reflection is one of the most powerful tools for mastering trading, investing, and decision-making. By consciously examining the motivations behind your choices, you can distinguish between decisions driven by transient emotions, ego, or deeper purpose. This weekly exercise allows you to gain self-awareness, identify behavioral patterns, and refine your approach over time, transforming trading from a reactive activity into a disciplined practice.

Why Reflection Matters

Without deliberate reflection, traders and investors often operate on autopilot, letting emotional impulses dictate actions:

- **Profit-driven decisions:** When financial gain is the sole motivator, traders may take excessive risk, chase volatile opportunities, or overtrade, often compromising long-term stability.
- **Ego-driven decisions:** Actions influenced by pride, fear of appearing wrong, or desire for recognition can lead to stubbornness, revenge trading, or ignoring evidence that contradicts beliefs.
- **Purpose-driven decisions:** Aligning choices with long-term goals, values, and meaningful objectives fosters patience, discipline, and sustainable growth, reducing emotional volatility.

Reflection helps reveal which of these forces is most active in your decisions at any given time.

How to Conduct a Weekly Reflection

1. **Set aside dedicated time:** Choose a consistent time each week to review trades, decisions, and emotional responses.

2. **Document your actions:** Maintain a journal noting the decisions made, the rationale, market context, and emotional state at the time.

3. **Analyze motivations:** For each decision, ask yourself:

   - Was this driven primarily by potential profit?
   - Did ego, fear, or desire for recognition play a role?
   - Was this aligned with my broader purpose and long-term strategy?

4. **Identify patterns:** Over weeks, look for recurring themes. Do you repeatedly act from fear during certain market conditions? Are there moments when greed overrides strategy?

5. **Adjust behavior:** Use these insights to recalibrate your approach, modify risk levels, and reinforce decisions that align with purpose rather than emotion.

Benefits of Weekly Reflection

- **Enhanced self-awareness:** Understand your emotional triggers, cognitive biases, and habitual responses.

- **Improved discipline:** Recognizing ego- or profit-driven impulses allows you to intervene before they compromise decisions.

- **Greater alignment with purpose:** Decisions increasingly reflect long-term strategy, values, and personal growth rather than short-term satisfaction.

- **Sustainable performance:** Consistent reflection fosters emotional resilience and a steady approach, even in volatile or unpredictable markets.

Key Insight

> *Mastery is not just about making the right trades it is about understanding why you make them. By dedicating time each week to reflect on whether your decisions are driven by profit, ego, or purpose, you transform self-awareness into a competitive edge, reduce emotional noise, and align your actions with sustainable success.*

Part VI

Strategic Applications

Chapter 23

The Smart Money Mindset

Markets are often viewed as a battleground between buyers and sellers, bulls and bears, retail and professional participants. Yet beneath the surface, a more profound dynamic is at play: the flow of capital orchestrated by institutional players banks, hedge funds, and sophisticated trading desks whose decisions shape price action over time. Understanding this "smart money" is not merely about tracking transactions or news; it requires thinking like these institutions, anticipating their strategies, and aligning your decisions with the forces that truly move markets.

This chapter explores the mindset of smart money, emphasizing psychological patterns, behavioral cycles, and strategic patience. By examining market behavior through the lens of institutional logic, traders and investors can identify asymmetric opportunities, reduce emotional bias, and position themselves in harmony with dominant market currents.

We will cover techniques for recognizing psychological patterns, understanding the role of narrative in market movements, and leveraging patience and contrarian thinking to gain an edge. Ultimately, adopting a smart money mindset is about elevating your approach from reactive speculation to informed, disciplined, and strategic participation in the markets.

23.1 Thinking Like Institutions, Not Individuals

One of the key distinctions between successful market participants and the majority of retail traders lies in perspective. Retail traders often operate as individuals, reacting to news, price movements, and personal biases. Institutions, by contrast, approach markets with strategy, discipline, and a systemic understanding of human behavior and capital flows. Thinking like an institution requires adopting a macro-level mindset while also focusing on execution, risk management, and psychological consistency.

The Institutional Perspective

Institutions do not trade for short-term gratification; they operate on multiple time horizons, balancing risk and reward across portfolios:

- **Capital Scale:** Institutions handle vast amounts of capital, which means their trades move markets and must be executed carefully to avoid adverse price impact.
- **Strategic Patience:** Institutional players are willing to wait for optimal setups, focusing on asymmetric opportunities where potential reward outweighs risk.
- **Process-Oriented Approach:** Decisions are based on predefined rules, risk limits, and probabilistic frameworks rather than emotional impulses.
- **Psychological Control:** Institutions cultivate emotional detachment, recognizing that individual price swings are irrelevant in the broader context of their strategy.

Common Retail Mistakes vs Institutional Mindset

Retail traders often fall into behavioral traps that institutions systematically exploit:

- **Chasing Trends:** Retail traders frequently buy high due to fear of missing out, while institutions take advantage of liquidity and volume imbalances.
- **Overreacting to News:** Emotional reactions to headlines lead to premature entries or exits; institutions assess the implications objectively.
- **Short-Term Focus:** Retail participants fixate on daily movements, while institutions plan over weeks, months, or even years.
- **Ignoring Risk Management:** Institutions prioritize exposure, hedging, and position sizing; retail traders often risk too much relative to capital and emotional tolerance.

Key Principles of Institutional Thinking

To align your mindset with that of smart money:

1. **Think in probabilities:** Institutions weigh potential outcomes and expected values rather than predicting certainties.
2. **Observe collective behavior:** Market patterns reflect the aggregation of participant psychology. Recognizing these allows for contrarian positioning.

3. **Prioritize process over outcome:** Focus on executing well-defined strategies consistently rather than obsessing over individual wins or losses.

4. **Stay patient and disciplined:** Wait for setups with a clear edge, resisting the temptation to act on impulse or fear.

5. **Measure and manage exposure:** Every trade or investment should be sized and timed in accordance with risk tolerance and strategic objectives.

Key Insight

Thinking like institutions means seeing beyond price charts and short-term noise. It involves understanding human behavior at scale, acting with patience, and making decisions rooted in probability, risk management, and strategic foresight. By adopting this mindset, you position yourself not as a reactive participant, but as a disciplined, informed player aligned with the forces that truly move markets.

23.2 Pattern Recognition Through Psychology

Markets are not random. Beneath the surface of price charts, volume fluctuations, and news events lies a consistent rhythm shaped by human behavior. Every rally, sell-off, or sideways move is a reflection of collective psychology, repeating emotional patterns that can be observed, analyzed, and leveraged. Understanding these patterns is not about predicting the future with certainty it is about recognizing recurring behaviors, biases, and responses that govern market dynamics.

The Foundation: Human Behavior Drives Patterns

Price movements are ultimately driven by people traders, investors, institutions each with emotions, fears, desires, and biases. Recognizing this fundamental principle allows you to interpret charts not as abstract lines, but as visual representations of human decision-making:

- **Fear and Panic:** Sharp declines often reflect herd behavior and emotional contagion.
- **Greed and Euphoria:** Rapid upward movements signal collective overconfidence and risk-taking.
- **Hesitation and Uncertainty:** Consolidation periods reveal indecision, reflecting conflicting impulses in the market.

By studying how these emotions manifest repeatedly, traders can anticipate potential reversals, breakouts, or continuations.

Identifying Behavioral Patterns

Key psychological patterns often appear across different timeframes and asset classes:

- **Reversal Points:** Fear-driven capitulations and greed-driven peaks create predictable turning points.
- **Volume and Momentum Surges:** Sudden spikes in activity often indicate herd behavior or institutional accumulation/distribution.
- **Support and Resistance Zones:** These areas are behavioral magnets where past emotions influence current decisions.
- **Recurring Cycles:** Market cycles boom, euphoria, fear, capitulation, recovery repeat because human psychology is largely consistent over time.

Recognizing these patterns allows traders to distinguish between noise and signal, improving timing, risk management, and decision quality.

Psychology-Based Technical Indicators

While technical tools like moving averages, RSI, or Fibonacci levels are widely used, their effectiveness is amplified when combined with behavioral context:

- **Volume as emotion:** Sudden volume spikes often correspond to emotional extremes rather than fundamentals.
- **Sentiment analysis:** Social media, news tone, and surveys provide insight into collective mood, helping confirm patterns.
- **Contrarian signals:** Extreme optimism or pessimism frequently precedes reversals, reflecting crowd behavior rather than intrinsic value.

By integrating psychology with technical analysis, traders gain a deeper, more actionable perspective.

Applying Pattern Recognition Practically

1. **Observe repetition:** Maintain a journal of emotional market patterns and your reactions to them.
2. **Map psychology to price action:** Identify where fear, greed, and indecision have historically influenced trends.

3. **Combine with risk management:** Use pattern recognition to set informed entries, exits, and position sizes.

4. **Test hypotheses:** Analyze historical cycles to verify if similar emotional patterns lead to consistent outcomes.

Key Insight

Price charts are not just numbers; they are mirrors of collective human behavior. By recognizing recurring psychological patterns, you can anticipate market tendencies, avoid reactive mistakes, and align your strategy with the underlying forces that drive price action. Pattern recognition through psychology transforms observation into actionable foresight.

23.3 Why Patience and Narrative Inversion Win

In markets, information travels fast, prices fluctuate, and crowd behavior often creates noise. Many traders succumb to impulsive decisions, reacting to headlines, short-term trends, or emotional swings. True edge, however, lies not in constant activity, but in patience waiting for asymmetric opportunities where the potential reward significantly outweighs the risk. Coupled with narrative inversion, this approach allows traders to anticipate market turning points and act when others are blinded by conventional thinking.

The Power of Patience

Patience is a strategic weapon in trading:

- **Avoiding noise:** Markets are filled with transient movements and emotional swings. Patience helps you filter out irrelevant signals and focus only on setups with high probability.

- **Waiting for asymmetric opportunities:** Not all trades are equal. By waiting for scenarios where risk is limited but upside is substantial, traders maximize long-term gains while minimizing exposure to losses.

- **Emotional control:** Patience naturally reduces impulsive actions driven by fear or greed, reinforcing discipline and mental clarity.

- **Compounding advantage:** Consistently entering positions with favorable risk/reward relationships allows small advantages to compound into substantial long-term growth.

Understanding Narrative Inversion

Narrative inversion is the practice of thinking against prevailing stories and popular assumptions in the market:

- **Crowd psychology:** Markets often react irrationally to narratives whether it is excessive optimism during a boom or pervasive pessimism during a crash. Recognizing these extremes enables contrarian positioning.
- **Contrarian edge:** By questioning the dominant story, traders can identify opportunities overlooked by the majority, such as buying during unwarranted panic or selling during irrational euphoria.
- **Pattern anticipation:** Many market cycles repeat because human psychology is consistent. Understanding prevailing narratives allows you to anticipate when sentiment may reverse.

Combining Patience with Narrative Inversion

The greatest traders blend patience with contrarian thinking:

1. **Observe the dominant narrative:** Identify the story that the majority of participants are following.
2. **Measure sentiment extremes:** Assess whether fear, greed, or denial has reached a peak or trough.
3. **Wait for asymmetric entry points:** Only act when the market presents a setup where risk is controlled and reward potential is high.
4. **Execute decisively:** Once the conditions are met, act with conviction, guided by analysis rather than emotion.

Benefits of Patience and Narrative Inversion

- **Reduced stress:** Fewer, higher-quality trades reduce emotional volatility.
- **Higher probability setups:** Waiting allows you to enter trades with clear advantages.
- **Enhanced long-term performance:** Consistently exploiting behavioral extremes compounds profitability over time.
- **Psychological resilience:** Acting against the crowd reinforces discipline and mental toughness, which are critical for navigating volatile markets.

Key Insight

Markets reward those who can wait patiently and think independently. By combining patience with narrative inversion, traders position themselves to act when opportunity arises, rather than chasing the crowd. Mastery is not about constant activity, but about disciplined observation, strategic entry, and leveraging the predictable patterns of human psychology.

Chapter 24

Reading Market Sentiment

Markets are not just driven by fundamentals or technical patterns they are reflections of collective human emotion. Every price move, surge in volume, or sudden drop represents a consensus of feelings: fear, greed, hope, or uncertainty. Understanding these underlying emotions the market's sentiment gives traders and investors an edge. It allows them to anticipate potential turning points, identify crowded trades, and position themselves ahead of the majority.

This chapter explores how to read market sentiment effectively. We will examine key indicators such as the VIX (Volatility Index), trading volume, and media tone, all of which provide windows into collective psychology. Additionally, we will discuss how narrative cycles dominant stories and market beliefs shape the flow of money, and how contrarian thinking can turn extreme sentiment into profitable opportunities. By the end of this chapter, you will understand how to interpret the emotional undercurrents of the market and translate them into actionable insights.

24.1 Sentiment Indicators: VIX, Volume, Media Tone

Market sentiment can be thought of as the collective mood of participants at any given time whether optimistic, fearful, greedy, or uncertain. While emotions themselves are intangible, their effects manifest in observable market metrics. Understanding and interpreting these indicators allows traders and investors to anticipate market behavior rather than react blindly.

The VIX: Measuring Fear and Uncertainty

The CBOE Volatility Index (VIX), often called the "fear index," measures the market's expectation of volatility over the next 30 days. It provides insight into investor anxiety and risk perception:

- **High VIX readings:** Elevated levels indicate fear and uncertainty, often coinciding with potential market bottoms or panic selling.
- **Low VIX readings:** Low values suggest complacency or overconfidence, which can precede market tops or irrational exuberance.
- **Contrarian application:** Traders frequently use VIX extremes to gauge sentiment overreaction, positioning themselves against the prevailing mood for asymmetric opportunities.

Volume: The Pulse of Market Activity

Trading volume reflects the intensity of market participation and can reveal the conviction behind price moves:

- **High volume with price movement:** Suggests strong conviction and can confirm the validity of a trend or breakout.
- **Low volume with price movement:** Indicates a lack of consensus and potential fragility in the trend, warning of false moves or reversals.
- **Volume spikes at extremes:** Often correspond with emotional climaxes panic selling or euphoric buying serving as contrarian signals.

Media Tone: Narratives in Action

The stories told by financial news, social media, and analyst commentary shape collective perception:

- **Positive media tone:** Can fuel optimism, FOMO, and trend continuation, often amplifying greed-driven behavior.
- **Negative media tone:** Heightens fear, selling pressure, and market pessimism.
- **Extreme consensus:** When all narratives align in one direction, it often signals overcrowded trades, creating opportunities for contrarian positioning.

Integrating Sentiment Indicators

To gain a comprehensive understanding of market psychology, combine these indicators:

1. Track VIX for volatility expectations and fear levels.
2. Observe volume patterns to confirm or question price movements.
3. Analyze media tone and dominant narratives for behavioral context.
4. Look for convergence or divergence among indicators to identify potential turning points.

Key Insight

> *Market sentiment is the invisible hand guiding price action. By reading fear, greed, and collective narratives through indicators like the VIX, volume, and media tone, you can anticipate moves before they occur, aligning your strategy with the true drivers of market behavior rather than mere price fluctuations.*

24.2 How Narrative Cycles Predict Money Flow

Markets are not driven solely by data, fundamentals, or isolated events they are shaped by collective stories and beliefs. Every rally or sell-off is often accompanied by a dominant narrative: a storyline that explains why prices are moving and influences participant behavior. Understanding these narrative cycles is crucial because they reveal the underlying psychology driving money flow and can help traders anticipate shifts before they become obvious in price action.

The Mechanics of Narrative Cycles

Narratives move markets because humans are story-driven creatures. Investors and traders interpret complex financial information through simplified stories, which creates predictable behavioral patterns:

- **Emerging Narrative:** A new idea or market theme begins to gain traction. Early adopters take positions, often quietly, creating subtle price changes.
- **Mainstream Adoption:** The narrative becomes widely accepted. Media coverage, social discussions, and analyst commentary amplify the story, attracting more participants. Prices rise or fall in alignment with the narrative.
- **Peak Consensus:** Overconfidence and euphoric behavior dominate. The narrative is taken as absolute truth, often signaling an unsustainable extreme.
- **Narrative Collapse:** Reality begins to contradict the story. Fear, doubt, and regret emerge, prompting rapid repositioning and reversals in money flow.

Examples of Narrative-Driven Money Flow

- **Tech Booms:** During the Dot-com era, the narrative of "new economy" profits drove massive inflows into internet stocks, creating unsustainable valuations.

- **Cryptocurrency Surges:** Narratives of decentralization and limitless adoption fueled dramatic inflows, often ahead of regulatory or fundamental considerations.
- **AI Investment Mania:** Stories about revolutionary AI potential can drive capital rapidly into related sectors, sometimes overshooting intrinsic value before sentiment corrects.

Interpreting Narrative Cycles for Trading

Understanding narrative cycles allows traders to position themselves advantageously:

1. **Identify the narrative early:** Recognize emerging stories before the crowd fully embraces them.
2. **Assess market participation:** Gauge whether the narrative is supported by sustained money flow or merely hype.
3. **Watch for consensus extremes:** When nearly everyone believes in a narrative, it may be time to prepare for a reversal.
4. **Align with contrarian signals:** Extreme sentiment often provides opportunities for asymmetric trades with favorable risk/reward profiles.

Key Insight

> *Markets are driven as much by stories as by numbers. By recognizing narrative cycles, you can anticipate where money is flowing and where it may reverse, allowing you to act before the majority reacts. Mastery of narrative analysis transforms you from a follower of price into a reader of collective psychology.*

24.3 Contrarian Thinking in Action

Contrarian thinking is the practice of positioning yourself against prevailing market sentiment. While most traders follow the crowd, reacting emotionally to fear or greed, contrarians seek opportunities where the majority has overreacted or misjudged the situation. Applied correctly, it transforms extreme sentiment into actionable advantage.

The Logic Behind Contrarian Thinking

Markets often swing to extremes because humans are prone to emotional biases:

- **Fear-driven selling:** Panics can push prices well below intrinsic value, creating buying opportunities for those willing to act against the crowd.

- **Greed-driven buying:** Euphoric rallies can inflate prices beyond reasonable levels, signaling potential shorting or risk reduction.
- **Herd mentality:** When everyone believes the same narrative, markets often overshoot before correcting, providing contrarians with asymmetric opportunities.

Identifying Contrarian Opportunities

Contrarian traders combine sentiment analysis, narrative cycles, and market indicators:

1. **Measure extreme sentiment:** Use VIX, volume, media tone, and surveys to identify overbought or oversold conditions.
2. **Assess narrative exhaustion:** Determine if the prevailing story is fully priced in and losing momentum.
3. **Look for liquidity gaps:** High panic or euphoria often leads to mispriced assets, which contrarians can exploit.
4. **Confirm with technical context:** Align contrarian entries with support/resistance zones, trendlines, or other technical confirmation to improve probability.

Practical Contrarian Strategies

- **Buying during panic:** Identify periods of mass fear where quality assets are sold indiscriminately.
- **Selling or hedging during euphoria:** Recognize when the crowd is irrationally optimistic and markets are near emotional peaks.
- **Gradual positioning:** Enter contrarian trades in tranches rather than all at once, allowing for confirmation of market reversal.
- **Risk management:** Set clear exit points and position sizes, as contrarian trades often face short-term volatility.

Key Insight

Contrarian thinking turns crowd behavior into an advantage. By acting when fear or greed dominates, you align with long-term value and asymmetric opportunity. The market rewards those who can see beyond the prevailing narrative, resist emotional impulses, and take disciplined, calculated positions against the herd.

Chapter 25

Behavioral Alpha Framework

Traditional alpha generation focuses on fundamentals, technical patterns, or market timing. While these are important, a deeper, often overlooked source of consistent advantage lies in understanding human behavior how collective biases, emotions, and psychological patterns influence market outcomes. The Behavioral Alpha Framework is designed to help traders and investors identify, measure, and exploit these biases systematically, transforming insights into actionable strategies.

This chapter explores three key components of behavioral alpha: recognizing recurring collective biases, designing psychology-based trade setups, and employing practical checklists to execute trades with discipline and rationality. By integrating behavioral science into your trading methodology, you gain an edge that is often invisible to those relying solely on numbers or conventional analysis. Mastery of this framework allows you to align your actions with the underlying psychological currents of the market, rather than being swept along by them.

25.1 Identify, Measure, and Exploit Collective Bias

Markets are fundamentally human constructs, driven by the emotions, beliefs, and biases of participants. Understanding these biases and their impact on price action provides traders with a powerful edge. The first step in creating behavioral alpha is to systematically identify, quantify, and act upon these collective tendencies.

Identifying Collective Biases

Collective biases are recurring patterns in behavior that manifest across groups of market participants:

- **Herding Behavior:** Traders often follow the majority, buying when others buy and selling when others sell, regardless of fundamentals.
- **Overconfidence and Confirmation Bias:** Participants tend to overweight information that supports their existing beliefs while ignoring contrary evidence.
- **Recency and Anchoring:** Market participants place undue emphasis on recent price moves or reference points, leading to skewed expectations.
- **Fear and Greed Extremes:** Emotional extremes cause overreactions, creating mispricings in both directions.

Recognizing these biases in real time requires both observation and historical analysis of market behavior.

Measuring Bias Impact

Quantifying the influence of biases helps determine actionable opportunities:

- **Sentiment Indicators:** Tools like the VIX, put/call ratios, and investor surveys measure market-wide fear and greed.
- **Volume and Price Divergence:** Discrepancies between trading volume and price action can signal biased behavior (e.g., panic selling or euphoric buying).
- **Media and Narrative Analysis:** Tracking dominant stories in financial news, social media, and analyst commentary provides a measure of crowd sentiment and conviction.

Combining these measurements allows traders to identify when emotions have pushed the market too far in one direction, creating high-probability opportunities.

Exploiting Collective Biases

Exploitation involves turning identified biases into systematic, repeatable strategies:

1. **Contrarian Positioning:** Take positions against extreme sentiment, buying during fear-driven sell-offs or trimming exposure during greed-driven rallies.

2. **Pattern Recognition:** Observe recurring emotional cycles and archetypal behaviors, such as panic capitulations or euphoric peaks, to anticipate reversals.

3. **Risk-Adjusted Execution:** Use defined entry and exit criteria to minimize exposure while maximizing potential reward.

4. **Continuous Feedback:** Maintain a behavioral journal to track bias recognition, trade outcomes, and lessons learned for iterative improvement.

Key Insight

> *Behavioral alpha is gained by seeing the market through the lens of human psychology. Identifying, measuring, and exploiting collective biases allows you to act with foresight, positioning yourself ahead of the crowd rather than reacting to it. In essence, your edge comes from understanding the predictable irrationality of others.*

25.2 Psychology-Based Trade Setups

Understanding collective biases is only valuable if it can be translated into actionable trades. Psychology-based trade setups leverage human behavior, emotional extremes, and predictable crowd patterns to create high-probability opportunities. Unlike conventional setups based purely on charts or fundamentals, these trades are designed around the recurring psychological tendencies that drive market moves.

Foundations of Psychology-Based Setups

Every trade setup based on behavioral insights relies on recognizing the underlying emotional drivers:

- **Fear-Driven Setups:** Panic selling often pushes assets below intrinsic value. A setup might involve identifying oversold conditions, extreme negative sentiment, and support levels to enter long positions.

- **Greed-Driven Setups:** Euphoric buying can inflate prices unsustainably. Shorting, profit-taking, or hedging can capitalize on these peaks when confirmation of overextension appears.

- **Herd Reversals:** When the majority follows the same narrative, a setup might involve anticipating trend exhaustion and positioning for reversal once sentiment extremes are reached.

Step-by-Step Approach

1. **Sentiment Analysis:** Use indicators like VIX, put/call ratios, volume spikes, and media tone to assess crowd emotion.

2. **Pattern Recognition:** Identify recurring emotional cycles such as panic capitulations, euphoric peaks, or revenge rallies that historically precede reversals or continuations.

3. **Trigger Confirmation:** Define clear signals that indicate the market is entering or exiting an extreme phase, including price action, volume anomalies, or divergence with sentiment indicators.

4. **Positioning and Risk Control:** Determine entry, stop-loss, and position size based on probability-weighted outcomes and personal risk tolerance.

5. **Execution and Review:** Execute trades systematically, then review performance against expectations to refine setups over time.

Examples of Psychology-Based Setups

- **Capitulation Longs:** During sharp market sell-offs, identify oversold assets where fear is driving prices below fair value. Enter gradually, with tight risk management.

- **Euphoria Shorts:** In high-flying rallies driven by greed and media hype, look for signs of exhaustion and divergence from fundamentals before initiating short positions or hedges.

- **Narrative Reversal Plays:** When a dominant story begins to collapse, anticipate the shift in collective behavior to position ahead of the broader market.

Key Insight

Psychology-based trade setups turn human emotion into a strategic advantage. By mapping predictable patterns of fear, greed, and herd behavior into structured trades, you can act before markets fully reflect the collective sentiment, capturing opportunities that remain invisible to those relying solely on conventional analysis.

25.3 Practical Checklists for Rational Execution

Even the best psychological insights and trade setups can fail without disciplined execution. Human traders are prone to emotional mistakes, impulsive decisions, and confirmation bias. Practical checklists provide a structured framework to ensure that every trade aligns with strategy, risk management, and behavioral analysis, minimizing errors and enhancing consistency.

Why Checklists Matter

Checklists serve as external memory and accountability tools:

- **Reduce Emotional Interference:** Following a checklist prevents impulsive decisions driven by fear or greed.
- **Ensure Consistency:** Each trade is evaluated against the same criteria, improving repeatability and reliability.
- **Identify Biases:** A structured checklist makes it easier to spot when emotions are influencing judgment.
- **Facilitate Post-Trade Review:** Recording adherence to checklists allows for systematic improvement over time.

Core Elements of a Behavioral Trading Checklist

A robust checklist should incorporate the following steps:

1. **Sentiment Confirmation:** Verify that the trade aligns with measured market sentiment extremes or narrative cycles.
2. **Setup Validation:** Confirm that the trade satisfies your psychology-based setup criteria (fear-driven, greed-driven, herd reversal, etc.).
3. **Risk Assessment:** Check position size, stop-loss levels, and maximum exposure against your risk tolerance and probability-weighted expectations.
4. **Entry Trigger Confirmation:** Ensure technical and behavioral triggers are present, avoiding premature execution.
5. **Behavioral Bias Check:** Ask: Am I trading based on strategy, or is emotion, ego, or wishful thinking influencing this decision?
6. **Exit Plan Defined:** Establish profit targets, stop-loss points, and conditions for adjusting the trade if the narrative or sentiment shifts.
7. **Record and Reflect:** Document the rationale, expected outcome, and actual execution to enable post-trade analysis.

Sample Pre-Trade Checklist

- **Sentiment Analysis Complete? ____**
- **Setup Validated Against Bias Patterns? ____**
- **Position Size and Risk Confirmed? ____**
- **Entry Triggers Met? ____**
- **Bias Check Completed? ____**
- **Exit Plan Documented? ____**
- **Trade Logged for Review? ____**

Key Insight

Behavioral alpha is only as effective as your execution. Checklists provide the discipline and structure necessary to convert psychological insights into profitable, repeatable trades. They act as a safeguard against emotional errors, ensuring that your decisions remain rational, objective, and aligned with long-term strategy.

Chapter 26

The Meta-Trader

Trading is often viewed as a battle against the market, charts, or other participants. However, the most profound edge comes from understanding yourself the mind that observes, reacts, and interprets the market. The concept of the Meta-Trader emphasizes self-awareness as a critical component of trading success, where observing your own thoughts, emotions, and biases becomes part of the system itself.

This chapter explores the principles of trading as a practice of self-mastery and spiritual growth. By integrating behavioral insights, mindfulness, and reflective discipline, you learn to transcend attachment to outcomes, respond rather than react, and harness both market sentiment and personal psychology. The Meta-Trader framework transforms trading from a mere pursuit of profits into a continuous journey of learning, adaptability, and conscious decision-making.

26.1 Observing Your Own Mind as Part of the System

The first principle of the Meta-Trader is the recognition that your mind is not separate from the market it is a participant, observer, and influencer within the system. Every thought, emotion, and bias subtly impacts your decisions, which in turn influences outcomes and reinforces psychological patterns. Developing the ability to observe your own cognitive and emotional processes transforms trading from reactive behavior into proactive strategy.

Why Self-Observation Matters

- **Awareness of Biases:** By actively observing your reactions, you can detect anchoring, confirmation bias, overconfidence, and other cognitive distortions before they affect decisions.

- **Emotional Regulation:** Noticing fear, greed, or FOMO in real time allows you to pause and respond intentionally rather than impulsively.
- **Pattern Recognition:** Self-observation helps you identify recurring emotional cycles, both in yourself and in market participants, providing insight into potential setups and reversals.
- **Mind-Market Alignment:** Understanding your mental and emotional state enables alignment with market conditions, improving timing, patience, and risk assessment.

Techniques for Observing the Mind

1. **Journaling:** Record not just trade details, but your emotions, thought patterns, and motivations during each decision. Over time, this reveals recurring cognitive tendencies.
2. **Mindfulness Practices:** Meditation and breathing exercises improve moment-to-moment awareness, helping traders notice impulses without acting on them immediately.
3. **Self-Inquiry:** Ask reflective questions such as: *"Am I trading this setup or my fear/greed?"*, *"What assumptions am I making?"*, or *"Is this decision aligned with my strategy?"*
4. **Behavioral Tracking:** Use checklists or scoring systems to objectively measure adherence to trading rules and behavioral discipline, reinforcing conscious decision-making.

Integrating Mind Observation into Trading

Observing your mind is not a one-time exercise it is a continuous process woven into every trade. By maintaining awareness of your own mental state, you can anticipate emotional pitfalls, adjust strategy in real time, and maintain clarity even in volatile markets. This meta-cognition transforms your role from passive participant to active observer, turning internal awareness into actionable market intelligence.

Key Insight

> *The market is a mirror of collective psychology, and your mind is a mirror of that mirror. By observing yourself as part of the system, you gain the meta-perspective necessary to act with clarity, discipline, and foresight, turning awareness into a sustainable edge.*

26.2 Trading as Spiritual Growth

Trading is often framed as a pursuit of profit, but at its highest level, it can be a journey of self-discovery and personal mastery. The act of engaging with markets exposes your deepest instincts, fears, desires, and biases. Approaching trading as spiritual growth means using this exposure to cultivate awareness, discipline, resilience, and wisdom qualities that extend far beyond financial success.

The Mind as the Marketplace

Every trade is a microcosm of your internal state:

- **Emotional Reflection:** Gains and losses act as mirrors, reflecting your attachment to outcomes, your ego, and your reaction patterns.
- **Testing Patience:** Markets challenge your ability to wait, act decisively, and tolerate uncertainty without succumbing to impulsivity.
- **Observing Attachment:** Recognizing how strongly you cling to positions, ideas, or narratives highlights areas for emotional growth.

Principles of Trading as Growth

1. **Self-Discipline:** Treating rules and checklists as inviolable structures builds integrity and self-trust.
2. **Embracing Uncertainty:** Markets are inherently unpredictable. Accepting uncertainty cultivates resilience, humility, and adaptability.
3. **Reflection and Learning:** Every trade win or loss is an opportunity to learn about yourself and the system. Documenting insights transforms experience into wisdom.
4. **Detachment from Outcomes:** Focusing on the process rather than profit reduces emotional reactivity and allows rational decision-making to dominate.

Practical Techniques

- **Daily Reflection:** Dedicate time to review not only trades but emotional responses, motivations, and reactions to market events.
- **Meditation and Mindfulness:** Develop sustained awareness of your mental and emotional state, allowing conscious choice instead of impulsive reaction.
- **Journaling Lessons:** Record insights about recurring behavioral patterns, attachment to outcomes, and personal growth moments for cumulative learning.

Key Insight

> *Trading is a mirror for the soul. By approaching it as a practice of spiritual growth, each market interaction becomes an opportunity to cultivate patience, self-awareness, emotional resilience, and disciplined action. Profit becomes a byproduct, not the sole objective, and mastery of self becomes the ultimate edge.*

26.3 Transcending Attachment to Results

One of the most challenging aspects of trading is the emotional weight of outcomes. Wins can inflate ego, while losses can provoke fear, regret, or revenge impulses. Transcending attachment to results means shifting focus from the outcome to the process, from what happens in the market to how you respond. This mindset fosters consistency, emotional stability, and long-term success.

The Trap of Outcome Dependence

Attachment to results often manifests in:

- **Overtrading:** Taking excessive positions to compensate for losses or chase wins.
- **Revenge Trading:** Reacting impulsively to recover from losses, often exacerbating mistakes.
- **Ego Inflation:** Letting profits boost overconfidence, leading to riskier decisions and ignoring established rules.

Recognizing these patterns is the first step toward transcending them.

Shifting Focus to Process

1. **Define Process-Oriented Goals:** Focus on adherence to trading plans, execution quality, and risk management rather than profit or loss.
2. **Track Behavioral Metrics:** Measure emotional discipline, rule adherence, and decision quality independently of market outcomes.
3. **Detachment Practices:** Use mindfulness, journaling, or meditation to observe market events and your reactions without judgment.

Benefits of Transcending Attachment

- **Emotional Resilience:** Detachment reduces stress and impulsive reactions during market volatility.
- **Improved Decision Quality:** Focus on process ensures rational, probabilistic decision-making, free from fear or greed.
- **Consistent Performance:** Over time, disciplined, outcome-independent trading produces sustainable results.

Key Insight

By detaching from outcomes and embracing process over results, you align your trading with rationality, discipline, and awareness. This not only protects you from emotional pitfalls but also transforms trading into a practice of mastery, where every decision reinforces learning and growth regardless of the market's immediate response.

Part VII

Conclusion Appendices

Conclusion: The Human Code of Markets

Markets are not merely mechanical systems of prices, volumes, and charts they are living reflections of human psychology. Every rise, fall, or sideways movement encapsulates the hopes, fears, greed, and regrets of countless participants. In this sense, every candle, bar, or price action represents an emotional imprint on the collective consciousness of the market.

This concluding chapter distills the insights from this book into the essential truth: mastering markets is inseparable from mastering oneself. Understanding human nature, recognizing cognitive biases, and observing your own mind are the ultimate keys to navigating financial markets with clarity, discipline, and strategic foresight. By internalizing the "Human Code of Markets," traders and investors can transform uncertainty into opportunity, turning emotional awareness into a sustainable edge.

Every Candle is Emotion

Every price movement in the market every candle on a chart is a manifestation of collective human emotion. Behind each bullish surge, bearish drop, or indecisive consolidation lies a complex interplay of fear, greed, hope, regret, and uncertainty. Understanding this emotional substrate is key to interpreting price action beyond the superficial patterns.

Decoding Emotional Signatures

- **Fear:** Sharp sell-offs, long wicks on the downside, and high-volume panic moves reflect widespread anxiety or uncertainty.
- **Greed:** Extended rallies, repeated breakouts, and euphoric buying indicate collective optimism or overconfidence.
- **Hope and Denial:** Prolonged sideways action in the face of negative news shows persistence of hope and cognitive bias toward previous highs.

- **Regret:** Sudden reversals or overreactions often emerge from participants trying to correct past mistakes, leading to amplified volatility.

Using Emotional Awareness in Trading

1. Observe volume spikes and price extremes as emotional indicators.
2. Cross-reference price patterns with sentiment indicators, news, and behavioral cues.
3. Recognize when emotion-driven extremes create asymmetric opportunities for informed trades.

Key Insight

Each candle is a story of human emotion. Mastering the ability to read these emotional signatures allows traders to anticipate potential moves, identify crowded behaviors, and exploit the predictable patterns created by collective psychology.

Mastering the Market Begins with Mastering Yourself

True mastery of financial markets does not come from memorizing indicators, chart patterns, or news events. It comes from understanding and mastering the most unpredictable and influential variable of all: yourself. Every decision you make, every trade you enter, and every position you hold is filtered through your own emotions, biases, and cognitive patterns. Recognizing this is the first step toward sustainable success.

The Inner Edge

Your psychological and emotional state is your primary edge. Traders who cultivate self-awareness can:

- **Identify Emotional Triggers:** Recognize fear, greed, overconfidence, and hope in real time to prevent impulsive decisions.
- **Control Reaction to Losses and Gains:** Avoid revenge trading, ego-driven risks, or euphoric overtrading.
- **Make Rational Decisions Under Pressure:** Detachment from outcomes allows probabilistic thinking and disciplined execution.

Developing Self-Mastery

1. **Mindfulness and Observation:** Regularly monitor thoughts, emotions, and reactions to trading stimuli. Awareness allows you to pause before acting.
2. **Process-Oriented Focus:** Emphasize adherence to trading rules, risk management, and quality of execution over short-term outcomes.
3. **Reflective Practice:** Maintain a journal to document trades, decisions, emotional states, and lessons learned. Over time, patterns emerge, providing insight into habitual behaviors and biases.
4. **Resilience and Patience:** Accept that losses, volatility, and uncertainty are inherent in markets. Cultivate a mindset that treats them as learning opportunities rather than threats.

The Meta-Perspective

Mastery of self transforms your perspective of the market. Rather than reacting to each fluctuation, you begin to observe the interplay of collective psychology and your own responses simultaneously. This meta-cognition creates clarity, reduces emotional interference, and allows for strategic, disciplined, and opportunistic decision-making.

Key Insight

> *The market is a reflection of human nature, and you are a part of that nature. By mastering your own mind emotions, biases, and reactions you gain the ultimate edge. Self-mastery is not just a tool for trading; it is the foundation for consistent performance, rational decision-making, and long-term success.*

The Laws of Market Psychology

Financial markets are complex systems, but at their core, they reflect timeless truths about human nature. Over decades of observation and study, certain behavioral patterns, cognitive biases, and emotional responses consistently shape market outcomes. These patterns repeat across time, asset classes, and geographies, forming the foundation for what we call the Laws of Market Psychology. Understanding these laws gives traders and investors a framework to anticipate market behavior and make rational, disciplined decisions.

1. Emotion Drives Price Action

Every price movement is rooted in human emotion fear, greed, hope, or regret. Market moves cannot be fully explained by fundamentals alone.

2. Fear is Amplified by Uncertainty

Uncertainty heightens fear, causing overreactions, panic selling, and herd behavior.

3. Greed Follows Success

Euphoric gains often trigger overconfidence, excessive risk-taking, and the pursuit of the "next big win."

4. Crowds Overreact

Market participants collectively exaggerate both fear and greed, leading to sharp swings and irrational extremes.

5. Patterns Repeat Due to Human Nature

Historical price cycles, bubbles, and crashes recur because human behavior does not fundamentally change.

6. Anchoring Influences Decisions

Traders rely on reference points (previous highs/lows) that can distort rational evaluation.

7. Loss Aversion Dominates Rationality

The pain of loss is psychologically stronger than the pleasure of gain, often leading to premature exits or holding losers too long.

8. Confirmation Bias Distorts Perception

Traders seek information that confirms their beliefs, ignoring contradictory evidence.

9. Overconfidence Skews Risk Assessment

Past success inflates self-perception and can result in underestimated risks and reckless decisions.

10. Herd Behavior is Inescapable

People tend to follow the crowd, even against their better judgment, especially under social pressure or uncertainty.

11. Hope Prolongs Losses

Hope can trap traders in losing positions due to the expectation of reversal.

12. Panic Spreads Faster Than Reason

Fear is contagious; a single trigger can cascade into mass selling.

13. FOMO Overrides Strategy

The fear of missing out drives impulsive trades, often at market tops or during rallies.

14. Markets Discount Everything

All available information is reflected in price; markets are forward-looking.

15. Emotional Memory Influences Future Decisions

Past gains and losses leave psychological imprints that shape future trading behavior.

16. Smart Money Moves Contrarily

Institutional participants often act opposite to prevailing retail sentiment, exploiting emotional extremes.

17. Markets Oscillate Between Fear and Greed

Emotional cycles are predictable; recognizing the dominant sentiment aids decision-making.

18. Trends Reflect Collective Psychology

Price trends are manifestations of prevailing sentiment and behavioral consensus.

19. Volatility Signals Emotional Intensity

High volatility indicates emotional extremes and potential reversal points.

20. Patience Wins

Waiting for high-probability setups minimizes emotional trading errors.

21. Self-Knowledge is the Ultimate Edge

Understanding your own biases, tendencies, and emotions gives you control over your decisions.

22. Overtrading is a Symptom of Emotional Weakness

Excessive activity often stems from fear, boredom, or ego rather than strategy.

23. Losses Teach Faster Than Gains

Mistakes provide the clearest insight into behavioral weaknesses.

24. Attachment to Outcomes Clouds Judgment

Detachment enables rational, probabilistic decision-making.

25. Market Cycles Are Human, Not Economic

Booms and busts are primarily driven by collective emotional responses rather than pure fundamentals.

26. Risk Perception is Subjective

Different traders perceive and tolerate risk differently, influencing position sizing and decision-making.

27. Contrarian Thinking Exploits Emotional Extremes

Opportunities often lie where sentiment is most skewed.

28. Consistency Outperforms Brilliance

Sustainable results come from disciplined adherence to process, not chasing brilliance.

29. Trading is a Reflection of the Self

Your market behavior mirrors your internal psychology, fears, and biases.

30. Complexity is Often Illusionary

Simple rules executed consistently often outperform complex strategies.

31. Markets Test Patience

Rational traders wait; impatient participants overreact and make mistakes.

32. Emotional Awareness Creates Edge

Recognizing your emotions in real-time allows you to prevent them from dictating trades.

33. Patterns Have Psychological Foundations

Technical formations reflect crowd psychology, not magic.

34. Euphoria Precedes Reversal

Excessive optimism usually signals a market top; panic precedes a bottom.

35. Losses Should Be Accepted Without Ego

Admitting mistakes early prevents compounding emotional errors.

36. Self-Discipline Amplifies Probabilistic Thinking

Following your rules strengthens rational decision-making under uncertainty.

37. Reflection Converts Experience into Wisdom

Journaling and post-trade analysis reveal patterns and biases that are otherwise invisible.

38. Emotional Contagion is Subtle

Even brief exposure to others' excitement or panic can influence decisions unconsciously.

39. Scarcity and Novelty Trigger Greed

New opportunities or limited supply provoke disproportionate emotional responses.

40. Pain and Pleasure Drive Decisions More Than Logic

Emotional responses override rationality in most trading situations.

41. Losses Can Be Constructive

Properly analyzed, losing trades provide valuable lessons for future opportunities.

42. Over-Reliance on Past Performance is Risky

Historical success does not guarantee future results; markets are dynamic.

43. Patience Cultivates Asymmetric Opportunities

Waiting allows you to exploit mispricings created by emotional extremes.

44. Markets Are Mirrors of Human Nature

Understanding collective psychology reveals likely market reactions.

45. Your Mind is Part of the Market System

Recognizing this prevents being an unintentional participant in emotional swings.

46. Emotional Regulation Determines Longevity

Sustained success depends more on controlling impulses than finding perfect setups.

47. Learning from History Enhances Intuition

Patterns of human behavior repeat; studying past manias and crashes builds foresight.

48. Flexibility Outperforms Rigidity

Adapting to new market conditions prevents fixed-pattern errors.

49. Fear and Greed Are Inescapable, But Manageable

Acknowledging these forces allows conscious navigation rather than reaction.

50. Mastery of Self Equals Mastery of Markets

The most powerful trading edge lies not in tools or strategies, but in understanding, observing, and mastering your own mind.

The Trader's Psychological Toolkit

Success in the markets is as much about mastering your mind as mastering charts. This chapter provides a comprehensive set of tools, journaling prompts, and frameworks to help traders understand their own psychology, manage emotions, and make disciplined, rational decisions. By using this toolkit, you can transform self-awareness into actionable strategies and convert psychological insight into a consistent edge.

Self-Assessment Tools

- **Emotional Baseline Tracking:** Record your emotional state at the start and end of each trading day to identify recurring patterns.
- **Risk Tolerance Questionnaire:** Evaluate your comfort with various levels of exposure, drawdowns, and volatility.
- **Bias Identification Checklist:** Note instances of anchoring, confirmation bias, overconfidence, and loss aversion in past trades.

Journaling Prompts

Daily reflection can illuminate patterns that are otherwise invisible. Consider incorporating:

1. **Pre-Trade Prompts:**
    - What is my rationale for this trade?
    - What emotional state am I in?
    - What is my risk and reward ratio?
2. **Post-Trade Prompts:**
    - Did I follow my plan? If not, why?

- What emotions influenced my decisions?
- What did I learn from this trade?

3. **Weekly Reflection:**
   - Which biases appeared most frequently?
   - Did I manage fear and greed effectively?
   - How can I improve my process next week?

Frameworks for Behavioral Mastery

The Emotional Cycle Map

- Track phases like fear, hope, greed, and regret in your trades.
- Identify your position in the cycle to anticipate emotional influence on decision-making.

The Process-Oriented Checklist

- Pre-define entry, exit, risk management, and emotional checkpoints.
- Follow the checklist rigorously to minimize emotional interference.

Cognitive Bias Neutralization Framework

1. Recognize the bias (e.g., confirmation, recency, anchoring).
2. Pause and question assumptions objectively.
3. Seek contrarian data or alternative perspectives.
4. Adjust the decision based on rational evaluation, not emotion.

Visualization and Mindset Tools

- **Mental Rehearsal:** Visualize trading scenarios, including losses and gains, to reduce emotional impact.
- **Meditation and Mindfulness:** Practice observing thoughts without judgment to improve focus and reduce reactive impulses.
- **Breathing and Stress Techniques:** Short exercises during trading sessions can restore clarity during high-pressure moments.

Key Insight

> *The Trader's Psychological Toolkit is not about avoiding emotions it is about understanding, managing, and leveraging them. By systematically tracking behavior, reflecting on decisions, and applying structured frameworks, you convert self-knowledge into a measurable, repeatable edge in the markets.*

Case Studies of Market Psychology in Action

Financial markets have repeatedly demonstrated that human psychology, rather than pure economics, drives extreme events. From historic crashes to modern manias, the patterns of fear, greed, hope, and regret manifest in remarkably similar ways. This chapter examines key historical episodes 1929, 2008, 2020, and 2021 to illustrate how collective psychology shapes market outcomes and why understanding these patterns is essential for traders and investors.

The Great Crash of 1929

The 1920s saw unprecedented economic growth, speculative fervor, and a cultural obsession with wealth accumulation. Investors, driven by optimism and greed, bought stocks without regard for underlying fundamentals.

Psychological Patterns Observed

- **Euphoria and Overconfidence:** Rapid gains reinforced the illusion of infallibility among investors.
- **Herd Behavior:** Retail investors followed institutional buying, escalating the bubble.
- **Panic Selling:** When prices began to fall, fear cascaded through the market, causing massive sell-offs and accelerating the crash.

Lessons

- Markets overreact both on the upside and downside.
- Emotional contagion can amplify small shocks into systemic collapses.

The 2008 Global Financial Crisis

The collapse of the housing market and the ensuing financial crisis exposed deep vulnerabilities in the financial system, magnified by human behavior.

Psychological Patterns Observed

- **Confirmation Bias:** Investors ignored warning signs, believing housing prices would continue rising indefinitely.
- **Greed and Risk Ignorance:** Complex derivatives and high leverage were embraced due to short-term profit incentives.
- **Fear and Herding:** Once defaults increased, fear spread rapidly, leading to widespread panic and systemic failure.

Lessons

- Overconfidence can blind markets to structural risk.
- Herding amplifies both bubbles and crashes.

The 2020 COVID-19 Market Shock

The onset of the COVID-19 pandemic created unprecedented uncertainty, triggering extreme volatility across asset classes.

Psychological Patterns Observed

- **Fear and Panic:** Sudden market drops reflected global anxiety and uncertainty.
- **Hope and Recovery Bias:** Rapid stimulus measures and optimism about recovery fueled a sharp rebound.
- **FOMO and Speculative Frenzy:** Retail participation surged, particularly in tech stocks and high-growth assets.

Lessons

- Emotional reactions can drive prices far beyond fundamentals in both directions.
- Rapid information flow accelerates collective decision-making and overreactions.

The 2021 Meme Stock Mania

The GameStop and related stock surges highlighted the power of social influence, online communities, and collective behavior.

Psychological Patterns Observed

- **Herding via Social Networks:** Retail investors coordinated through online forums, amplifying price movements.
- **Greed and Overconfidence:** The desire for rapid gains fueled speculative trades.
- **Fear of Missing Out (FOMO):** Investors jumped in late, further inflating volatility.

Lessons

- Social dynamics can override traditional market fundamentals.
- Emotional triggers such as envy, greed, and FOMO are timeless drivers of market extremes.

Recurring Psychological Themes

Across all these cases, common patterns emerge:

- **Euphoria and Overconfidence** drive bubbles.
- **Fear and Panic** drive crashes.
- **Herd Behavior** accelerates extremes.
- **Cognitive Biases** distort rational evaluation.
- **Hope, Denial, and Regret** influence both the buildup and unwinding of market cycles.

Key Insight

> *Market psychology is remarkably consistent across time and asset classes. By studying historical episodes, traders and investors can recognize emotional signatures, anticipate crowd behavior, and use psychological insight as a strategic edge. Human nature is the constant; market conditions change, but the patterns of behavior repeat.*

Recommended Readings & Resources

Understanding market psychology and human behavior is a lifelong journey. The following curated list of books, articles, research papers, and online resources provides a foundation for traders, investors, and curious minds seeking deeper insight into behavioral finance, trading psychology, and the timeless principles of human nature that shape markets.

Behavioral Finance Classics

- **"Thinking, Fast and Slow" by Daniel Kahneman** Explores the dual-system theory of human cognition and how biases impact decision-making.
- **"Misbehaving: The Making of Behavioral Economics" by Richard H. Thaler** Chronicles the evolution of behavioral economics and practical market implications.
- **"Behavioral Finance: Psychology, Decision-Making, and Markets" by Lucy Ackert & Richard Deaves** A comprehensive academic treatment of behavioral finance principles and market applications.

Trading Psychology and Market Behavior

- **"The Psychology of Trading" by Brett N. Steenbarger** Offers practical tools and strategies to manage emotions and optimize trading performance.
- **"Trading in the Zone" by Mark Douglas** Focuses on mindset, discipline, and developing the mental edge in trading.
- **"Enhancing Trader Performance" by Brett N. Steenbarger** Combines behavioral science with actionable insights for professional traders.

Human Nature and Decision-Making

- **"Influence: The Psychology of Persuasion" by Robert B. Cialdini** Examines the principles of social influence and human compliance that affect financial and social decisions.
- **"Predictably Irrational" by Dan Ariely** Explores systematic human biases and irrational behaviors in economic contexts.
- **"The Wisdom of Crowds" by James Surowiecki** Investigates collective decision-making and how group psychology shapes outcomes.

Case Studies and Market History

- **"Extraordinary Popular Delusions and the Madness of Crowds" by Charles Mackay** A timeless exploration of market manias, bubbles, and speculative behavior.
- **"Manias, Panics, and Crashes" by Charles P. Kindleberger** A scholarly analysis of financial crises and recurring behavioral patterns.
- **"Irrational Exuberance" by Robert J. Shiller** Combines economics, psychology, and historical analysis to explain bubbles and investor behavior.

Online Resources and Communities

- **Behavioral Finance Journals:** Journal of Behavioral Finance, Journal of Economic Behavior & Organization.
- **Trading Psychology Blogs:** TradingPsychologyEdge.com, Steenbarger.com, TraderFeed.
- **Educational Platforms:** Coursera and edX courses on behavioral economics, finance, and decision-making.

Key Insight

The best traders and investors combine practical experience with continuous study of human behavior. By learning from the pioneers of behavioral finance, psychology, and historical market events, you cultivate both the analytical and intuitive understanding necessary to navigate markets with confidence and discipline.

The Future of Human Nature in AI Markets

As artificial intelligence and algorithmic trading increasingly dominate financial markets, a pressing question emerges: what is the role of human nature in this new era? While machines can process vast amounts of data, detect patterns, and execute trades with lightning speed, they lack the emotional depth, intuition, and consciousness that define human decision-making. This chapter explores the interplay between human psychology and AI-driven markets, the limits of algorithmic reasoning, and the enduring edge of conscious insight.

Will Machines Outsmart Emotion?

AI systems excel at identifying statistical patterns, optimizing strategies, and executing trades without the interference of fear, greed, or overconfidence. Yet, market disruptions, black swan events, and sentiment-driven phenomena often arise from human behavior itself. Algorithms can react to historical patterns, but they cannot fully anticipate the spontaneous, irrational impulses of millions of market participants acting collectively. Human emotion, paradoxically, remains both a source of vulnerability and a strategic advantage when understood and harnessed.

Human Intuition vs Algorithmic Reasoning

- **Pattern Recognition:** While AI detects correlations and trends across vast datasets, human intuition excels at recognizing emergent behaviors that may not yet be statistically significant.

- **Contextual Understanding:** Humans integrate macroeconomic, geopolitical, and psychological signals into decisions, often considering factors that are intangible or unquantifiable.

- **Flexibility and Creativity:** Unlike rigid algorithms, humans can adapt rapidly to unprecedented events, drawing on imagination and experience to devise novel strategies.

The Last Edge: Consciousness

Even in markets dominated by machines, consciousness remains the ultimate differentiator. Self-awareness allows traders to:

- Recognize emotional biases and cognitive distortions in themselves and others.
- Develop probabilistic thinking that incorporates uncertainty and ambiguity.
- Exercise judgment in situations where data is incomplete, misleading, or contextually complex.

In essence, the human mind can perceive nuances and narrative shifts that AI may overlook. By combining analytical rigor with psychological insight, traders can maintain a decisive edge even as algorithmic strategies proliferate.

Key Insight

AI may revolutionize speed, scale, and efficiency in markets, but the essence of trading understanding human behavior, anticipating emotion-driven moves, and exercising conscious judgment remains inherently human. The future belongs to those who master both technology and the subtleties of human nature.

www.ingramcontent.com/pod-product-compliance
Lightning Source LLC
Chambersburg PA
CBHW050525240926
51846CB00003B/695